run

scream

unbury

save

LITERARY MEMOIR

Katherine McCord

Autumn House Press
pittsburgh

 Autumn House Press receives state arts
funding support through a grant from
the Pennsylvania Council on the Arts,
a state agency funded by the Commonwealth of Pennsylvania, and the
National Endowment for the Arts, a federal agency.

ISBN: 978-1-938769-18-4
Library of Congress Control Number: 2016955596

For Tom, Greta and Adi

And thank you to Ryan and Christine and Michael and Autumn House: I just plain don't have the words yet, but I will.

PREFACE (SEE ALSO, "PREFACE," PAGE 60 (OR THERE ABOUT))

I'm not kidding, go to page 60. Or, if you are like me and anything out of the ordinary makes you nervous while you feed on the out of the ordinary, go to the next page and think about it, going to page 60, first. And, if you are even more like me, don't go to page 60 because you don't like being told what to do and just go to the next page. Especially because you abhor people who think they're so "creative" when they are not but just in your face, which doesn't make them creative. And you want everything streamlined to art. Art or nothing. And you think going to page 60 where the preface is can in no way be art. Finally, if it makes you happy, I wouldn't go to page 60 either. Too risky. And I don't want to fail you. And if you don't go to page 60, nothing will be lost. I promise. You'll get there when you get there. Srsly. Proceed as normal.

(There may be some cross-referencing in this book. Okay, there is. But it will fall off. And sometimes I'll later contradict what I've said. But all in good fun. Like when I talk about guns. I was raised around them. Sometimes I remember shooting a lot. Sometimes not. Stuff like that. Add in that we are kinda all-or-nothing in our family. My "family of origin" if you're into that. More news: I was the "lost" child. ☺ If you're not into that or don't know what I'm talking about, it's not your loss. You'll still understand. Also, sometimes there will be entries with the same name. I believe in organic learning. So things change. Also, too, forgive me, but don't move forward from here unless you're all in. That is, you are good at letting go. As in, just read, People, read. Zone. It's better than any drug I've ever found. It's probably one of the reasons I'm still alive. Lastly, yep, I consider you my friend. Big deal, that! My friends must hear me bring up some of the same things over and over again. In various 12 step programs we're told it's a forgetting disease. Whatever disease we currently have. I figure living is just forgetting, over and over again. Okay, next page.)

This page is purposefully blank so you can take a breath. I like breaths between prefaceyish type things. I let it go through my whole body, like I did with the preface and with prefaces I'm not talking about boring intros that explain various criticisms or why this author has edited the following as such. I'm kind of burned out on all that kind of study. Saturated would be the better word. So take a breath and let it fall through your whole body. Then proceed. I will stop talking now so you can do it.

Since the page before was supposed to be blank I'm trying again. This page will really be blank. I am now shutting up. Now we are blank.

Promises, promises. Welcome to my world, part one. Actually, no one promised me anything. It's sorta been the other extreme. I've gone after anything that can promise me nothing. Such makes more sense to me.

ABOUT THE CIA   The phone rings after my on-air interview. It's Mom. She was listening along with my aunt and uncle. Well, she says, your dad wasn't identified via a test for the CIA like you said. He signed up while in the army. Or something like that. (This is news to me.) Terry (my uncle), she says, said to tell you if you ever want to know anything call him. Apparently he once bailed your dad out of jail. One night, she goes on talking over my guffaws, your father and his buddies, fellow CIA, wherever we were at the time overseas, got drunk and made plans to scale the Chinese embassy wall. You were tiny. *Little*. Then she goes, I was out of my mind with fear. Well, yeah, I say, amazed by these details I didn't have BEFORE I WROTE MY BOOK for which I was interviewed. For which, let's just say, I'd done my own intense interrogations and scaling of walls. But I guess things are forgotten (by me) only to surface at extraordinary times, like just after you've done a gig on national radio and unknowingly gotten stuff wrong, ABOUT THE CIA.

LITTLE   And I am: stomped on, confused, somewhat weepy, having stopped myself, barely, from shooting off swear-word-full emails to my superiors. Because I'm in the middle of an online class where I'm not getting paid to learn a new "platform" from which I will teach my students. Let's just say for the non-digitally appreciative the last hours have been another source of frustration. Without getting on a soapbox, we can recognize truth. Especially because of this course, I'm not so slowly losing faith in my fellow humankind thinking digital is the way to go while not admitting the real reason: it's cheaper, you can hire lots of adjuncts, make them pay for all things computer, continue the tradition of keeping them from getting their due pay and benefits and consequently upgrade every football field at all universities keeping the trend of turning colleges into non-free-thinking staffed businesses. Let's also add that it's 2 degrees outside. I've spent the day under that eerie certain slant of light (thank you Emily Dickinson) of late winter trying to imagine what the "resource" of "chatting" has to do with anything. Even if I could access it. Even if I wouldn't get shaming emails for not being able to access it. Even if I could link, paste, tweet, hashtag, trend, hack, crash, post, copy, embed this "tool."

TOOL   He's such a *tool*, one of my students said describing some literary character. As in bad. A *playa*. And I thought it apt because tool has that sound to it. Here, I'll explain: I had this dream where the only way to get "to town" was climbing/walking/sort of balancing/straddling these interlocking crossing-each-other's-paths trails made out of nets. And it wasn't the only thing precarious. Apparently our home was a drug house, as in Big Motherfucking Drug Lord house. And we, some dear friends and I, lived in constant fear at said dwelling while doing various tasks (removing tile in a bathroom?) that various drug lords would ask of us. We were in Mexico. Go figure. But the deal was we were haunted by wanting to get home, as in our real homes. In the U.S. At one point, I imagine or am able to get to a phone in said town that I've climbed precarious nets to get to, to call my husband. It's him, it's really the one I'm married to in real life. I'm alive, I whisper into the phone. Not, I'm in Mexico and help. Not, I'm in Mexico and I think the town is or my surroundings look like, just, I'm alive. And then, Click, I leave the rest up to him. Next scene. I'm in, with same friends but now said husband has joined me, some kind of camp at the base of some kind of mountain I've frequented in other dreams. (I swear, I'm not trying to lose you.) The camp is kinda history museum/kinda girl scout away camp/kinda place of reckoning. To up the ante, a dear former professor who recently killed herself and left her literary estate to me (in real life) is with us. When said husband accidentally drives our van into a pond, she remains happy

5

enough and that night sleeps soundly in a cot in some last-minute shelter we've found. At this point though, I've lost real husband again, he's with our real girls and we've lost our cell phones. It turns out this camp is much bigger than we thought. What permeates my every move is I've lost any grasp on being important to my family, them needing, valuing me, wanting to look for me, while I'm well aware that the presence of my very fragile friend is, well, extremely fragile. Her situation weighs heavily. Is unresolved. And I carry that feeling of almost, maybe or in the future having lost my family because of what exact reason I don't know. But it stays. All waking day. Until I come here and acknowledge it. Not that acknowledging it takes away the pain. In fact, the pain of the whole thing is more real. But while I'm feeling it, I'm aware that the truth of it, such circumstances, aren't. Or perhaps I've made choices to make my awake circumstances real: I don't live in a camp or a drug house away from my family. My friend is dead, it's true. And I live with how much I loved her, what she meant to me, the world is at a loss without her, that I replay her last weeks in my mind trying to unearth what I'd do if I'd known every day. But the deal is I couldn't have changed her trajectory if I tried. Because I did try. Even if I didn't put her demise before my family (and saying this out loud hurts the worst), I remained her friend to the end. That is, I turn to my student and for real say, Bless you for finding the exact right word.

TRAJECTORY On the website for one of the schools where I teach is something like "Tips for How to Handle Shooters." I guess it's obvious, although I'm not knocking them for feeling it needed to be said: barricade, hunker down, be quiet, turn the lights off. This being old news to many of us who have children or recently had in public schools, so are the terms, lockdown, code yellow, orange, red. A practice that has been emphatically taken up by my daughters, operating at some level of terror since the day of. Because my girls are the generation which will replay the trajectory of planes within their psyches forever. The morning after 9/11 at my daughter's preschool, despite that many of their parents, my daughter's included, kept them from having seen the footage, several children gathered around a tower they'd built out of blocks. It was already teetering when they took up their toy planes. Not out of anger or rambunctiousness or randomness. Not out of being kids. It was methodical. *A reenactment.* As if they could play it back.

REENACTMENT   Whether I truly understand
what I just learned, that a widget is a tool, I don't know. But
at least they have something in common. Perhaps widgets will
feel less alone. Tools too. With the arrival of widgets in my
mind, comes the hard, true fact that the digital age is meant
to keep me slammed. As in, whammo, a huge stack of papers
filled with T.S. Eliot like references—poems whose allusions
are cryptic, cross-referenced to footnotes, endnotes some editor
put in to try to help us rise out of the muck, gets slammed,
cartoon style, on the pavement in front of you, the whole
thing like a class I took as an English grad student where we
literally were set off on hunts in the library, that lasted days,
a set timer about to explode. Eventually unshowered and on
no sleep looking for some innocuous but creepy, archaic and
cryptic, esoteric yet preposterous reference within a reference
within a reference clue, confirming how antiquated my vision:
Notice there's no laptop in that pile. And that this leaning
tower will need brand new shelves. That the whole clusterfuck
(some grad students actually accused other grad students
of purposefully losing the keys to the kingdom, references,
microfiche, slides, card catalogue cards, maps, albums, tapes,
filmstrips that lead to the actual line on some page in some
unheard of place (book we needed)) is just a reenactment that
does nothing and everything, including teach what it means to
be insane.

SHELVES   My husband is really into shelves. He's constantly asking us, as in me and oldest and youngest daughters, if we need shelves. He'll even point to a wall where he envisions them. The problem is none of us, save youngest daughter when she's in an accommodating mood, like shelves. Or I guess I should say, none of us *use* shelves. Like a duckling imprints just after it's hatched, my girls did the same in terms of shelves. They were born. They looked up. And they took notes. Okay, they said, we get it, she likes things clean but out, where she can see, but certainly not orderly. She's no hoarder, this one, but she's into piles; upon arrival the youngest looked to the oldest and they both knowingly nodded their heads. Piles are the key to life. Drawers should be mostly empty. If it's in a drawer, take it out and examine it. Think of what it would be good for, clean it, organize it in terms of its parts— make sure they work, or maybe not—and then zen-like, place it in a random space, on top of a pile in a basket, on top of a pile on the dining room table, on top of a pile near the kitchen sink, on top of a pile on the toaster, on top of a pile on any flat surface, no matter how narrow, wide, as long as it's a few inches or more off the floor. Or, for god's sake, pass it on. Or better yet, let it slightly and daringly hang off some edge, if there is an edge left for it to hang off of. While my husband, the girls' father whom they respect and enjoy, places his things on shelves and not in random order, he's pretty much given up on the rest of the house. Sure, various Christmases he's gifted us orderly wood or steel desks (whicker or rattan or anything

bamboo not being sturdy enough, he convinces himself
in weaker moments, for all that they'll hold) for which he
promises to layer shelves above, getting all wise about various
kinds of brackets while we drift off. And sometimes we "let
him" (although in the early days, while there was still time, I'd
pack up the girls and flee somewhere for the afternoon, finding
the process more than spiritually draining) get the drill out
or haul in a monster box he's strapped to the roof of the car,
a crate containing parts of something for which he has high
hopes. But it doesn't mean, and I emphasize this, that in the
end we'll understand. Or he will. For example, at the moment
all my oldest daughter's clothes, everything she owns that's not
in the laundry or strewn through her car, are in a horse trough
I bought and painted brown with metallic sparkles. And
this idea came from our youngest who lived with a different
horse trough for clothes for most of her mid teens but has
now graduated to giant baskets she's labeled in a moment of
confusion and that she now ignores. And each morning, the
horse trough in the hallway outside our room, he manages past
it, between teetering piles on the banister, often to retrieve a
clean towel from a cool, giant, old, handwoven, I've convinced
myself, basket I found at a consignment store and placed in
what we call the room no one will label, out of some kind of
fear or anxiety it seems, the place I've given to, lately, write,
and the look on his face while he's doing this is, well, no less
than angelic (sorry, Tom), soft like he's just stepped out of a
really good dream.

BAMBOO　It's happened four times. First on the way to one of the schools where I teach. Next in a scrabble of abandoned woods. Third via a report from the wife of my husband's colleague's son. Near their house, he had shouted. Rare as the abandoned lot near their development in which it stood. It was my parents who bought the furniture in Africa and Nepal in the 60s and paired it, once home, and the brass tables, oriental rugs, elephant tusks carved into birds and other furnishings made from exotic woods with crystal, glass-topped marble and antiques, silver and expensive rifles hung on the wall, that, minus of course the guns and Persian carpets, jangled in unison whenever you walked through our living room, office or den. While I never once, while growing up, that I can remember, totally consciously entertained thought on the irreparable damage of colonialism or the exploitation of the people, animals and lands of the "third world" (as if they are assigned, after capitalism and communism, to a separate planet?), now delegated the term, "developing countries" (but to what? one might ask, the "developed" countries standards of consumerism?), or what, exactly, my aloof but protective, distant but loving, well-read and thoughtful but complicated alcoholic father whom I loved dearly did for the CIA. It just reminded me I was lucky—born abroad, overseas, that we'd been far, around the world in fact, and when. With the dismantling of my parents' marriage, that part of our lives it seemed I no longer knew or really sought. And the furniture was eventually sold. Probably, good riddance, I confusingly, as an unwieldy, hurting and ignorant teenager turned rebel of something I didn't quite know myself well enough to put a finger on (and now long for) thought. But not when it concerned the country I was bred to, my proclivity beginning in childhood, I'd read what I could find in school libraries for the inevitable reports which consisted of re-wording encyclopedia entries with their categories, like people, animals, government, crops. My nation, at least the one I was born to, only recently opening its war-torn weary doors, the clinic where my sister and I entered this world leveled, no more exotic to its beyond words traumatized true citizens and former boy soldiers than the charred remains of a village or city or its crumbling concrete blocks.

AFTER RESEARCHING THE DIFFERENCES BETWEEN CONCRETE, CEMENT AND CINDER BLOCKS

All oblong, these gray skies are heaviest winter, early spring and late fall. As if the summers of my life were newly stacked and sealed within.

It's like camping, I once told my sister, laughing, about our first residence, a tiny rectangular former military barrack made out of cinder blocks, our university family housing house planted in the very southwest of our Southwestern state. Newly married, we just put a rug over the drain in the floor. And a few nights past, having signed the contract but still locked out, easily pried loose an almost malleable screen frame and climbed indoors.

CAMPING   In fact, I was a girl scout, if a more skeptical one basically just along for the ride, given there wasn't much for a girl to choose from via school, not that I would have picked differently, in the early 70s in the Midwest. But when I hit early adolescence I ditched. Fell back on the wonder my mother and father had imbued us with and taught us, like staring transfixed among the thick old aboveground roots of our oaks, gone wild lilies of the valley planted by someone way previous and acorns in various states of decomposing, their hats flung off among the roots. It wasn't just the business of camping, I guess, as an adult who miserably failed at matching 3D boxes with their flattened, laid out counterparts on the SATs and GREs, that caused me to falter, halt, before my imagined state of standing among parts in a spastically moving sea—poles needing to Go somewhere, flaps and pieces wrongly affixed. Stakes. All for sleep. In the name of sleep. When I already have so much trouble. With sleep. And the apple doesn't fall too far from the tree. I can see all four of us, my husband and our girls, wandering among our flashlights' transposed beams, knotted with nobody's moons.

SLEEP (SEE ALSO, "IN THE MIDDLE OF THE NIGHT" AND "CROP CIRCLES")   My mother, a devout Catholic, also considers varying theories concerning (the concepts of) psychics, extraterrestrial life and ghosts. She's neat like that, my artist mother. Complex. A matrix. A virtual walking contradiction. Like when out of nowhere today she referred to extraterrestrials, trying to remember the word, have it click, clink or thunk into our conversation, not just like a puzzle piece, but also in terms of sound, timing, a relish she, I and my sister share (especially when we are telling stories). Extra something, she had said. Exterr, Extraterra. Unable to recall either, spending much of my days half in and out of my body, part here, someone, I claim, not totally planted on this earth, under or over the radar, that is, even if within the domain, sphere of activity, borders, not detected, my dad used to say, I let (it, the word) go. I know what you mean, I agreed. She was circling a possible scenario for a missing airliner. At a loss myself, I threw in the Bermuda Triangle to show her I was on the same plane. After all, we were technically brainstorming for all these normal seeming people (like us, "regular Joes," "everyday folk") who disappear or account, limn and chronicle getting whisked from their beds, later reporting, I knew they weren't trying to hurt me, just interested. Curious. And, once targeted, always earmarked, so that the beings often come back. I've watched my mother considering being transfixed, too, in front of "documentaries" or documentaries that I hope are really documentaries about such things as crop circles,

15

Bigfoot and Nessie in the Loch Ness. I mean, I was often at her side. (Or, later, at least on the phone hearing her watch.) Watching her watch. Watching myself watch. Wondering over and hypothesizing about my father, where the hell he was. Still, inevitably, one must go to bed. And while I'm not about ever to tell a scary story (they always seem just way too cliché and pointless), and as an adjunct college English professor turned down an offer to teach Poe, it's easy enough to lie awake and have your children know you do, so that you ingrain in them this turmoil over and entertaining of insomnia despite your desperation not to, so that soon they accompany you. And though I don't (often) think about being transported on a starship without my consent or waking to our backyard mowed, tamped down really, into some giant, divine, bizarre design you can only fully realize from the air, I wonder. I mean, I'd love, circumstances embracing, to live on a farm where the animals are rescued, given the love they deserve. . . .

CROP CIRCLES (SEE ALSO, "IN THE MIDDLE OF THE NIGHT" AND "SLEEP")

We had "cover for action," the former CIA operative says at her reading/talk at Politics & Prose bookstore in Washington, D.C. I think of crop circles, golden, in the documentary where the MIT kids plan, then carry out, their version, in the middle of the night, trying to prove the out-of-this world theories wrong and covert theories right. Or not. Just seeing if they can do it. They fail, but not quite. They go to plan B where things are so loud and bright it would wake any farmer to come down to his porch, see what the ruckus, miracle, was about.

IN THE MIDDLE OF THE NIGHT
(SEE ALSO, "CROP CIRCLES" AND "SLEEP")

There are only so many ways to try and get back or get to sleep. When the world is off, better, strange. You aren't the same person. Sometimes you are a sharp, more creative self. Sometimes you just suck. Logic, rationality, you consider, hype. You wish on a star. You do not wish on this.

YOU (SEE ALSO, "YOU II")   It's not that Salinger, my huckleberry friend, is unknowable. A case of going after secrets. It's his *characters*, that become me, you. Which are so true. I mean, how else does it happen, in a high school, library, in the rural Midwest, what seems long ago? First there is Sylvia, her bell, someone got away with putting in a stack, then a *Catcher*, somehow, gets through.

YOU II/POSTMODERNISM/ MODERNISM (SEE ALSO, "YOU")

Everyone seems apt to be flat. Memoirs intentionally holed. Charlie Brown at Halloween hauling rocks à la Sisyphus. In something you aren't capable of describing or fail to, choose to shoot yourself in the foot with on your comprehensive exams, going all gorgeously feminist in love with a man (you still love) and wanting to have his kids right now (which you did) via Cat's Eye by Margaret Atwood your tunnel vision for that supposed test and plan (and hope and are living) to live the rest of your life that way, as in somewhat wonderfully confused and limping: But not in a sheet, a costume or as a ghost.

So you didn't do well on the exams because of one fucker.

Everything else turned out.

SISYPHUS   When I was a kid, my father, fresh out of the CIA, interviewed for a job as a Sky Marshal, the Sky Marshals part of a program put into effect by President Kennedy as a result of a rash of hijackings via the U.S. and Cuba and later within the Middle East. I remember my dad that particular bright round day in a gray suit leaving for his interview. As if I look through a spyglass. When the job implodes shortly thereafter in the early 70s because the program was ratcheted down, then cut and the men disbanded, only to climb the government's priority list in the mid 80s and subsequently be spun down again, my father has already left. A job for the CIA in Langley not an option, we're told later, because he can't be tied to a desk, and that's not why he joined the ranks in the first place, which I get about him, get. But there's also land bought somewhere in the beginning in Virginia, we're in addition later informed, an "investment" he liquidates now, I'm assuming, to survive, one I can't help but to have linked to the future, a house, it's mirror, mystery, the climb to not ever knowing what he thought.

BB'S, MAGICAL REALISM I, LISTS, REPLY ALL (SEE ALSO, DR. SEUSS, MAGICAL REALISM II)

Since you asked, I imagine on Bimini Island there won't be a chance to use "reply all," in that we won't be able to get an internet connection and may not even be able to access our phones. Our youngest wants to visit. Or maybe it's me mostly. Yeah, it's mostly me. Along with New Orleans. She says something like, I don't know. There's a reason. I have some kind of connection, maybe a past life. She provides us with a list of places there we'll see—a pre-Civil War plantation (we're all hoping with no slave history) originally run by women (we're all hoping of color), the House of the Rising Sun . . . you know, real upbeat. But it's okay, she says, if we can't go. With the hefty weight of our somewhat known world and pretty much unknown worlds in tow, I play out both spots in my mind, our child's potential preter-past, my paternal grandparents, both she never met and one she feels she has a strong connection with, her great-grandparents who honeymooned there, a port from which they left for a cruise, in the early 1900s and brought back intriguing pen and inks of famous relic haunts, one being a near 200-year-old wrought iron gate. Then I picture us on Bimini, with its newly-surfaced out of the "slime of the ages" partly exposed Road to Atlantis (see Edgar Cayce), Fountain of Youth (see Ponce de León) and Healing Hole (I have no idea whom to see—but headed there, you get to behold the spot where Martin Luther King, Jr., penned his Nobel Peace Prize speech), having just hit the Coral

Castle, on Florida's southernmost mainland coast, a structure
that defies the odds, in that it was secretly constructed in the
early 20th century, nights, by a slight-of-build guy, in honor of
his girlfriend who evidently ditched him and whom he seemed
to have plans to win back, and no one can without doubt figure
out how he harvested and carried the coral stone with limited
crude equipment, alone, while my husband hits the computer
to nail down a budget, book tickets, carve out an agenda and
I eventually cave, am shored up by an oncoming migraine,
given the hove up meaning, for us all. And so that when later,
out walking, recuperating, bleary-eyed, on a damp path, I
sight a bright, almost neon, green bead and slipping it in my
pocket, thinking talisman but what the hell of I don't know,
I'm startled when my husband says pellet. But I had a BB gun
as a kid, I tell him, standing the small rifle in my mind on end,
opening the shaft, cupping my hand to carefully guide the
copper specks in. To shoot apples. And I digress, but here, I'm
convinced, in that I've given this a lot of thought and it must
be addressed, finally, now, is why. Their abundance. We had
two huge trees that, most especially one, without fail, year after
year, would unleash. Pound the ground with bumper crops all
late summers and falls, and the major chore of my sister and
me was to "pick up apples" as if it were that innocuous, pounds
and pounds of them, wheelbarrows and wheelbarrows, that we
dragged to the back of, to us, our acreage (big yard) to dump
and let further rot, bees flying to accompany our (my) unheard
or at least ignored screaming, the sweet spoil of apples, not
overtaking the spent can smell of meant for indoor use insect
spray I, the scaredy-cat, might, making things way harder,
try to protect us (me) with, when it was available, if we could
find it in the myriad, random recesses of the cooled, exotically

furnished but seemingly absent parent (do you blame them?),
ebony-stained-wood-floors-overlaid-with-oriental-rugs house,
that in itself was its own little adventure, I thought unknown
to our parents, like it would make any difference, trying to
alter our eventually begrudgingly accepted kid fate, usually,
just before the end.

Then there was the blowing them up.

With firecrackers once Fourth of July appeared on the horizon,
that is, the stands opened, a month or so before the night would
commence. Like it wasn't our somewhat distantly directing
dad's idea that we gratefully took up. Each evening he would
drive us to the nearest place (en route for beer), a kind of front
to back narrow but elongated width hut wedged and propped
over a sliver of a creek at the side of the road, keep us supplied
with Blackjacks, Smoke Bombs, Snakes and Punks. So that all
day we could shred apples, in the blaze of Midwestern heat,
our selves turning black with the smoke, powder, ash, blow
apples, sometimes red-turning but mostly green, to smithereens
and by day's end mirror the seemingly oily, glinting-to-almost-
purple-iridescence of baby black Medusa snakes or my dad's
favorite, tiered, Kali's arms.

Because we were thought worthy of our unmanaged summer
days. Times galore.

That or our parents were just somewhat distracted by their
own reveries and artistic endeavors.

Or the haze of deep feelings and battles we were trying to ignore.

Given what I have and will continue to explain.

(Oh, and since I fear getting it wrong in terms of other perspectives (I'm totally going to lose in general here, but, hey, why not give a shout out to recognizing I maybe misremember in other eyes) and thereby being cheerfully revised, I should note: sometimes our much younger escape artist of a brother was forced (by bossy us or halfheartedly by our parents) to "help," "pick up apples" (for as long as we could corral him). And later he became the best lad firecracker aficionado of all. Along with his best friend cousin, that is . . .)

And the "talisman"? It's not a true bullet. More like a keyed up bee.

FOUNDLING, FOUNDRY, SKEET AND COPPER

I know it sounds ominous, but it's not, the instinct never among us to handle my father's guns on our own. I rarely remember shooting, other than, as explained, and maybe the replica of an antique pistol Dad made, his hands around mine as I aimed, or once at a sports camp an unfamiliar gun for which I got in line but felt fear and disdain, high powered, bulky, new. I was probably ten. My father's goal mostly just wanting to roam, on foot, or in his old open Jeep. I only remember one dinner eating pheasant steeped in some kind of velvety gourmet wine sauce my mother made. While there is a story that one of my father's buddies brought him a live pheasant that the family friend had accidentally trapped. Dad let it go. Also, curiously, our beloved Irish setter was gun-shy, a wonderful dog for whom we moved out of city limits, cooked for, welcomed before every fire, on every bed, who ran the neighborhood free and each Christmas wore, attached to his collar by my parents, an epic, bright red bow, ragged by nightfall above the blue tinted snow. And I remember my dad shooting skeet, those light copper colored disks of hardened clay, seemingly silky and soft to the touch, shattering midair. It's cool out, probably late fall, the closing edge of a silvery day. We're at the Country Club. If we want to take a turn, last chance, my father will brace us for the kickback, shout pull, guide our final aim.

DISDAIN   Let's just say grad school is a great place
for the dysfunctional. A workshop can bring out the worst. I
wore everything I had on my sleeve. And was good at remorse.
People, I was afraid. And getting into a prestigious program
doesn't keep your peers from hate. Maybe it just exacerbates.
Along with faculty who are struggling just the same. Here's
one example among many. Picture a circle of people similar to
the ones in nursery school. But seemingly elevated by tables,
chairs. A famous poet to my right. An empty spot between.
He has rock star long hair girls are known to want to touch.
He definitely gravitates toward the breed. Maybe actresses
in training, such that you think red carpet when you hear
their names. Next to them I was, point blank, a fool. A fellow
student writer's poem before us, tied up, you could almost
hear it bleating on the page. While class members discussed
the author would be poet who hadn't yet showed up. What's
her occupation? the rock star asked. I believed I knew. I think
she said she "negotiates large contracts," I offered, so rare for
me to utter a word. What that meant, whether she was in
human resources or sales, I didn't have a clue but was trying to
be true to what she'd said. And in the only moment the rock
star poet would ever glance my way, he turned, just slightly,
so. Derision? All I know was that he mirrored the contempt I
felt for myself on his long oval face. For a split-atom moment
in the proceedings of before-workshop mingling, the most
awkward time for those of us desperate for some guidance as
to what to say, do, even a metaphorical train wreck with its

rules, run, scream, unbury, save, being less stressful, certainly more dire and worth-it/life-purpose real for such pain. And to be fair, I know I subconsciously brought it on myself. But how to make it stop? It was years before I recognized there was no absolute one key. That's the lamb. And that it still bleeds. That's the train.

RUN, SCREAM, UNBURY, SAVE

I don't expect to hear from my husband until late. Something about a proposal. I imagine detection, from the sky or space, of bombs. One child asleep, the other gone, I watch the car across the street pull up. The kid driving it, no, it's the dad, gets out, fear riding like a plane, low, almost constantly, above my head. When it kicked in to live like this, I don't know. I began wrestling with such in my first book. Like the Etheridge poem today, one that my students love, "Feeling Fucked Up," it's a matter of tone.

SPRING   Like if Fitzgerald's Daisy were winter,
having just absconded, this would be her detritus, the first
hot day of spring, mailboxes knocked over by snowplows,
one propped up on a curbside chair, roads, in part, reduced to
rubble, cavernous potholes, overhead jets sunk in cloudlessness,
a toilet, as if by a bad child, newly shot up dry weeds: I'm
driving. I'm stopping. I'm texting my sister. I think she gave
us up for lent, I say, referring to our mom. And, I can feel her
mind. She's holding back, being reserved, she was on her way
to a retreat. My sister texts back hahahahaha. Then, Why, what
did we do? We're too busy, I say, none of it matters. You know,
all the "commotion." And then, I dunno, but I'm no longer the
better behaving offspring. And since you haven't been for a
while, tag, you're it.

"BEAUTY IS TRUTH, TRUTH BEAUTY,"—THAT IS ALL YE KNOW ON EARTH, AND ALL YE NEED TO KNOW

1. TRUTH—How once, in your clothes, you swam with your sister and friend in a river and your parents, you don't think, knew. How you all held onto branches, the river deep and black and cold. And how once you couldn't stop crying, as a child, a little older now, and saw yourself outside yourself. So it didn't hurt, or you didn't know why it didn't hurt, or you didn't know, exactly, for whom you cried.

2. BEAUTY—When I found my husband, then boyfriend, the doors open to let in the full-on spring breeze, during his first grad school finals week, having turned over the previously soaked-with-rain recliner he found by a trashcan a few months before. The stereo blasting over the raucous dissonance of spring birds, I shouted, What doing? He was fixing the lever on our one chair. Knowing my boyfriend was a hardcore no-buts-about-it student, as in serious, as in a doctoral program in physics, I knew he was stressed. Beyond stressed. In that he was in a weird state I'd witnessed few others totally in, myself included, before. It's called happy, but ironically a kind of glad just before one upends, that is, goes a little crazy, whereby there is often a certain lightness about a person, they seem/ are, for lack of better words, unhooked, as if swimming in that light, as if the burning, the smoldering, is no longer consuming them. And it wasn't until he produced. Got that lever working, probably a few jaunty trips to the hardware store later, accompanied by his whistling, as in completed, done, the in-your-hands result, that the chair couldn't have gone flatter under his back, that he allowed the pre-exam face-yourself-in-the-mirror stormy darkness to do its thing, tie him back to this darn world.

Or there's this: Driving Midwestern lit up highways with our mother to or from somewhere I fail to remember, late springs, all summers, early falls, it wasn't at all odd for her to shout something I didn't understand and swerve the car to the side of

the road, having spotted some cache of wildflower, blooming
weed, perfect for drying, or some over-the-gorgeous top
arrangement for an upscale cocktail party. Maybe producing
scissors she'd jump out of the car where we were welcome
to join her and harvest, throw down the hatch in the back,
and toss everything in. Or, how Christmas seasons, various
supplies laid out for the taking, once wooden ornaments for
painting, once all sizes of Styrofoam balls, loads of material
scraps, shiny pearls you could push a decorated pin through,
ribbon and rickrack, glue, so that anyone at anytime could
produce as many as one wanted glinting and wrapped in
motley-hued material Christmas ornament balls, or, this: the
year we macramed at all hours of the night, in front of the TV,
or in the car to our away-from-home respite, gentleman's farm,
we'd, the female members, slip the beginning open-ended
knot over our big toes and produce spiraling plant hangers,
one after another in various patterns, woven with scads of
wooden carved-in patterns or animals beads, or this: the year
of craft kits. Where, standing in aisles we'd pick from boxes
like the one advertising flowers molded from wire and dipped
in some kind of liquid that would, in the air, film and dry in
many-colored, tie-dyed petals you could arrange into flowers
and then bouquets, meanwhile the Tole painting lessons,
where at the start of each project we'd select from a store of
finished products hand done by our instructors—planters,
sleds, old umbrella stands—anything you could imagine
painting on with this quaint technique of fashioning scenes
with such things as flowers, mushrooms, animals, ivy, fairies,
leaves, halfway realistic looking, done carefully with oils, or
this: my father helping me extract the candle from my metal,
star-shaped, found-in-the-recesses-of-an-art-shop-with-my-

mother mold, not long after watching him, fighting his yearly seasonal affective disorder bout, take up fashioning bullets that looked instead like thick, old, imperfect, impenetrable, dusty, opaque marbles, so that nightly, the day of dun cold behind us, I stood next to him at the stove as he poured the molten lead into a cavity, and one after another, eased the cooling, heavy, ore-ish silver orbs onto a paper plate; and there's even this: my brother's favorite, as in, not, as in scaring the hell out of him and make an early weird memory he as an adult won't let go of, when, unsuspecting, he'd rounded a corner, our trip to the dark side probably around Halloween already started, our kit already delved in, various stages of purposefully rotting and drying, our favorite to torture, apples, lined up. Eyes gouged, noses dangling, nature taking its course. Because we'd run out of other ideas, in the background my father's much scarier moods and alcoholism taking him down, trying to ruin us, my mother, herself barely withstanding the weight of us, having chosen to or been chosen to, no matter what in the end, directing us, my sister and me, our brother still too young, but, trust me, not far behind, his own materials soon to be model airplanes, music, wood, toward what was possible on that perpetual scale of human beauty, both hers, and, sometimes, his.

BROTHERS (NOT MINE)

So was it Sexton who famously referred to the po' biz as the business of words? The term has connoted various things for me over the years. But one strain: I don't like it, the business part. It's not the prose or the poems I cram into an overstuffed file I slam into a dinosaur of a filing cabinet on its last legs, rusty in part, near a window where the sunlight filters through dust, the barely moving drawer doing that awful screech. And this is not metaphorical, even in the digital age.

Years ago, the famous newspaper article, letter to the editor, whatever the hell it was, about a famous writers "conference" or extended "workshop" where famous poets and other famous writers would gather to teach a little less famous students who had jockeyed to get in, caused a storm. In it the author, a former "student," described the typical week. The famous poets sat on the famous porch of that famous place while the students themselves plunked in a hierarchy tried to get up on that very male famous porch. The author described the students as slinking around in nearby bushes, looking for a way in, or should I say, on that porch. The whole scene makes me feel queasy, sick. And not because of what you think:

Put me in a room with esteemed taking-on-that-role writerly men and women and I'm probably doomed. I won't ask anything of them. But I will spill my drink. Sputter out something that nears a mix of Greek and French when one doesn't know Greek and French. My need (hopefully, has been) that great.

Doing research on Plath through the Rare Book Room in the library at Smith I came across one of her cover letters, really a note, for a submission of poems to a male editor. It was signed, "Love, Sylvia." In other words, it was laid bare.

Let's mix it up: Let's give a Thomas Hardy character a tragic flaw that's her gift. You are reading and knowing, as always, these characters are going down. There's no way things will turn around. There's no wedding that's going to go off, especially for the impregnated out-of-wedlock character. And there's no country to move to. There's only doom, People, doom. Still, you hang on. Watching things spiral down the drain. Then, behold, someone says something beautiful, *is* something beautiful: It's enough to keep you reading. Because, despite how it may seem, you aren't a masochist. In fact, you're all about hope. I don't care what anyone else says, why else would you do this?:

Social mistake after social mistake, I wake up flat on my back in a ravine.

Like van Gogh, his ear in his hand. Of course it's a terrible, bad thing. But it was because he felt it, People, loved, not that he'd traded it, for pain. (Yeah, sure, he was also probably *a little* insane.)

"VINCENT (STARRY, STARRY NIGHT)"

And on another note, they just found one of your paintings (unknown/lost) in an abandoned safety deposit box somewhere overseas.

How could we be so lucky?   When you weren't.

DR. SEUSS/MAGICAL REALISM II

(SEE ALSO, BB'S, MAGICAL REALISM I, LISTS
REPLY ALL)   It's all about the trees. I can see them
magically (one by one) springing up in my hand (poof, poof,
poof). Pouf. An elephant spots a bird's nest not big enough for
the bird. The bird has an excruciatingly long neck that pains
her but helps both of them, individually, see: <u>One Hundred
Years of Solitude</u>. Who hasn't cried a river, lake, a world?

MIRACLE/POOF (SEE ALSO, "VINCENT (STARRY, STARRY NIGHT)")

She says she slept with a loaded gun under the bed. What kind? I ask, pen in hand, having pulled the car over. A pistol, she says. Oh, I bet Dad loved that! I say, trying to make her laugh. It was after we got robbed when we were in Nepal, she rushes on. I slept in your room, the two of you. Your dad was doing shift work. Oh, I say, imagining the gun lit up, on the floor under the standard army gray raised frame of the bed, my sister and I, variously sprawled and tucked, in what would be immaculately laundered, soft, exquisite, probably white eyelet bedding, while ticking off my list to see if I can spark her memory concerning one of the front companies the CIA used in Coral Gables and Miami at the time. Later I realize from this conversation I've gathered more than I thought, one of the few benefits of the job, I jokingly tell my students.

Off and driving to figure out where I'm supposed to go, I'm remembering more of what she said, like, Everybody drank. A lot. And then my secret ignites: The one where I imagine all of it as if it hadn't gone fallow. He stopped drinking. I got married in my hometown, St. Joe. He couldn't, she'd said. They (therapists) told me it was never going to happen. Toward the end of the conversation, He married the wrong person. He was really supposed to marry Ann. He wanted to be a gentleman farmer, I offer, something she's said. Yes, she agrees, but I wanted no part of it. The loneliness, she says, being out in the boondocks.   Oh, I say, then, Oh. . .Oh.

RADICAL   Feeling I should be in the "r's" by now
even though this isn't
alphabetical.

It's (kinda?, supposed to be?, depending on your perspective?,)
radical.

SHORT LISTS are not long lists, so I ask the "assistant" on the other side of the email explaining my book hasn't made it, Is there a Long List? She thinks I'm totally serious, and emails back, (Hell) No.

HELL (SEE ALSO, "PURGATORY,"
"CROSSING THE RIVER STYX. . . ." (IN OTHER
DICTIONARIES, ENCYCLOPEDIAS, ETC.))
is, I'm happy to say, not a contender (in this).

STEEL(E)   When with my sister, we saw a guy dressed up like bacon but I couldn't figure out he was bacon until I ask my sister and she says, Bacon? But I really can't quite understand her saying, Bacon? until she says it a few times because we're laughing and I'm deaf in one ear. And then I ask her, But why? like she would know, like she has the answers to all things. And she says, I don't know. At least I think that's what she says because at this point I'm laughing so hard I can't see.

And this: I witnessed same and only sister crash her car at an odd intersection that I'm never or rarely or just this time at when I didn't know it was her but jumped out to help her, this woman I don't, until after I've helped her from her totally smashed car, truly see.

And this: Steele was my father's middle name and given that I sort of remember he was named after someone I research the name and find the person he was named after but then my mother says she's not sure he was really named after him but that my grandparents, Dad's parents, just may have liked the name of this long ago family friend and frequent business partner. So that then it seems even more like such a heavy name, a "hard" name, "Steele," even though it's not the same spelling of steel, I see steel. So stuck there in the middle of David and McCord it seems like, Whoa, we are expecting you to be made of steel. But that's just my perspective, not really knowing my grandparents for sure in that way before they died. Nor do I have my dad's perspective, in that he maybe never felt that way, so I guess this is a caveat to all of you, us, me, a reminder, late in the game, to beware, about perspective and that it's important because of how someone else may, to survive, need to be, I mean, see.

SAYINGS AND WASPS It occurs to me
that I've done that thing where one saying gets confused with
another like I heard the other day—double edged street (a
combination of It's a two-way street and It's a double-edged
sword) but not totally. I had used "mud on my face" or
something close and realized later I wasn't sure if that was
right. So I find out it's mud in your eye or egg on your face
and that maybe I thought mud on your face because mud on
your face is in "We Will Rock You" by Queen and that little
tune was big in high school, in that we would sing/chant it
on the bus heading to a game as a cheer sort of, clapping and
stomping our feet so that, rhythm and all, it was pretty early
on tucked way down within my psyche. But while doing
this research I come across all kinds of people arguing about
the meaning of Queen's lyrics, specifically, mud on your face
and I kind of ignore it as having any kind of deeper meaning
because I like the pretty literal, it seems to me, "egg on" and
"mud in" meanings of the sayings. That is, Brian May writes
and Freddie Mercury sings, "You got mud on yo' face / You
big disgrace / Kickin' your can all over the place," as in (to me)
you are young, in the street, playing kid games like Kick the
Can and you don't know enough or better, yet, how it is not
about just trying to have fun all the time. For example, like,
with wasps. Because surprisingly or not wasps have consumed
a lot of time in my life and I suspect people's lives in general.
For me, I seem to be allergic to their sting. As in one time,
while pregnant, I got stung while unknowingly brushing away

one that had landed on my arm or flew in near it while I was, as usual, staring off into the distance. And my arm ballooned up. But I just thought that normal, when getting stung by a wasp. I mean, who do you know that's gotten stung by a wasp (not a bee) and told you about it? So a couple days later, at the doc for a prescheduled, usual monthly check in/up concerning my pregnancy, he seemed alarmed, taking ahold of my arm, saying, WHAT is that?! Pointing to the puncture wound. And, totally caught off guard, I shrugged my shoulders. And I don't know why. And he let it go. And my arm went back, after a week or so, to its normal size. But now I think about that darn wasp poison shooting through my blood/veins past my baby and wonder over the effect it might have had. Yes, she was born a normal healthy kid, but still. So I examine the origins of The Wasp in my life and it seems a large portion of my childhood summers were spent, along with my sister and brother, fleeing from, avoiding rooms with, screaming beneath wasps. They seemed to especially love our den, one of the only air conditioned rooms in our house and one where my parents had taken out the ceiling so that the inside apex of the room, a giant upside down V they painted white, careened above. And that's where the wasps would go if they weren't stupidly crashing incessantly into various windows. And there were a damned lot of windows in that room. So that they wouldn't Stay There or Sit Still or better yet Stay in Their "Rooms" way up and Settle Down in a crook so we could try and rationalize they weren't there. Because, it seemed to us, they were mad. Always mad. Swooping down to get us, kids, and, as noted previously concerning bees and apples, we found ourselves always/next in search of that precarious (probably nearly or totally empty but not thrown away giving you the idea there is at least enough spray to kill a wasp (or a bee but our bees were always in factions so bees) so you can watch your show or read in peace and only to find out at the most inopportune time that the contents of the can are just enough to piss off the wasp(s) even more) can of bug spray. And god forbid you try the old fashioned more brazen way and slap the wasp out of its seemingly pissed off misery with a rolled up <u>New Yorker</u>. Because you would miss and then you were in true, unadulterated real hell. At least that's how it seemed. The wasps were always going to win. And only when near crying because it was so hot outside and you had nowhere else to go, your parents, as usual, benignly absent doing adult things, the sun beating down on the plains you loved as in part of your Being/Psyche, but, hey, had no choice but to live on, and you just wanted to rest in a chair in peace would you Finally go after a wasp or make your older sister do it. Which was what we did. So that today it seemed Way, way too easy, People. The wasp inside doing its thing banging away head first at the back sliding glass door, I did *my* thing and opened said door thinking, as always, it would make its way out. But of course it didn't. Stupid wasp. Stupid stupid ugly wasp. So that I had to do the next obvious thing, whether logical or not (since we, of course, don't own a can of bug spray), I grab the can of oven cleaner. And I pray. But here's the thing, it's EASY, People. The wasp goes down without a count. Yeah, I use about half the can of oven cleaner. And yeah I disregard the fact that the spray will probably eat off the varnish on our wood floor (where most of the can ends up). But still. I *easily* swoop the dead guy up with a wad of paper towels after "he" within seconds stops moving and throw him in the trash and clean up the remaining flood. The whole thing takes under a minute. And I'm stunned. And I think, maybe it's because I kept my eyes open while spraying. And then I think, maybe it's because I didn't spray with my eyes closed and then run (with my eyes open) but kept at it. And, then, maybe it's because I'm an adult? And, then, maybe it's because I HAD to be less afraid because I'm an adult. And, then, Maybe it's that I more hated that wasp with a vengeance (than I was terrified—I've got Stuff To Do, I'm adult after all) even if I thanked him for his service of being a wasp before I tossed him in the trash.

ADDENDUM/APOLOGIA/ERRAT(A OR UM) AND ADJUNCT/ADJUNCT PROFESSOR (LATER THAT (THE PREVIOUSLY NOTED) DAY)

Yeah, so, oven cleaner not only eats varnish but paint also and it turns white plastic things a sordid brown. I'm waiting for my husband and kids to notice. WHY DON'T I KNOW THESE THINGS?!?!!!

Speaking of lists (of lists):

1. I Also Suck At
(not writing about my writing, for example)

2. (Other) Weird Things That Happen When I'm With My Sister
(too many to list)

3. Weird Things That Just Happen
(like today, for example, real summer, I go outside, and sitting there is a huge black crow perched on the pretty much short white post that is a part of what holds our mailbox up, in that I mean the giant bird engulfs the post and is all freelance and/or on loan casual, like, no big deal, I'm just sitting here all stark and everything when it's not even cool and fall and gray or eerie out, so that I think immediately, oh, god, some kind of sign, talisman, foretelling, omen of something not good)

So I am one. An adjunct prof. The worst of the definitions for "adjunct professor" being "assistant, low-level, subordinate, lower in rank or importance." A definition for adjunct being basically the same thing: "an expression in parentheses." But, I mean, why define it, the ubiquitous plastic bag of our current post-secondary educational system, the elephant in the room (except for to torture myself and say how we're all in this together, lovingly pet the elephant, unhook the bag from the wind or a tree and recycle it)? Doesn't it go without saying, despite the fact that I chose this, in that I don't want to be a full prof anywhere (kinda, long story) so I piece full-time work together through a couple universities? Otherwise it's too-too hard. Too many faculty meetings and too much backstabbing. Not like it doesn't still go on. But at least now I don't have to hear about it (mostly). And I'm a woman. So I'll get paid less regardless, promoted less regardless, published less regardless, valued less regardless. My writing voice (that's not just me, me but us, us/you, you and way wonderfully weirder even than that—if I'm writing well), what I write about, and how, will mean less, regardless, so it's just easier this route. For all parties involved. I'd rather have the energy to write the truth. And let the scholars fight the battle. Not that I'm not a scholar. I've given my fair share of time to research and study. And still do. In fact, a great deal more than I'd like to admit. But I figure, if you want to be a mother, you have to choose, if you are made up with the likes of me and not famous. Nope, it's not right. But that's the truth. So here's the best of the definitions of "adjunct." Okay, I lied, there isn't a "best of." Certainly not a best. So here's an "eh": "a group of words that form a constituent of a sentence and are considered as a single unit." Onward, People, onward. One (female) foot in front of the other. And, lastly, a true definition, possible ad, written for/by me/us: Adjunct Professor: Usually female. Most often hired to teach writing but as a male would teach writing, given that post secondary educational situations were established by the white male status quo at the time and we've followed that tradition once established. Needed because leaders of university/colleges are not in the business of paying their teachers (thereby hiring more fulltime talent with the better pay, potentially kinder circumstances because of potentially more women at the helm, sabbaticals and health insurance so said faculty can publish/do research that enables them to keep their jobs and receive tenure that comes with the position of non-adjunct professor) but in the biz of channeling institutions' money toward things like football stadiums.

(P.S. Source(s) for definition(s)? Smart people driven by institutions is my guess: Vocabulary.com, et al.)

JUST SAYING AND A SHARK IS A SHARK IS A SHARK   I think I see Mary

Oliver (you know, Mary Oliver, the celebrated poet?) in the
Miami airport. I can't help it. I do it. I ask her, Are you Mary
Oliver? And she says no but she has *read* Mary Oliver (rare
considering Mary Oliver is a poet) and we laugh, good feelings
exchanged. Good feelings continued from us, my husband
and one daughter, having just been to Bimini (you know, the
Bahamian island, 50 miles east of Miami, in the path of the
Gulf Stream, where Martin Luther King, Jr. wrote his Nobel
Peace Prize speech (we see the actual place in the middle of a
mangrove forest near another place called the Healing Hole
that you have to swim to, even our little boat too small to fit
the passageways between mangroves)). It had been a goal of
ours to get there but because of dredging going on we were
unable to snorkel (on another day trip) above the Bimini Road,
also called a part of the Road to Atlantis that Edgar Cayce
predicted would surface out of the muck and mire (I think
he called it slime of the ages) and did. Maybe around 20 years
ago. So before I know it, we've agreed, in a conversation I
couldn't quite hear, the dazzling, inebriating, intoxicating sun
reflecting off the wildly turquoise and bath water warm water
feet away, to snorkeling with sharks instead. Now, I know
there are "kinds" of sharks. And I know about media hype.
And I know about the odds of getting struck by lightning.
And yet it is freakin odd to me that I nodded my head and
followed behind my enthused husband and daughter *toward*
those sharks. AND casually stepped off the boat (as snorkelers

are taught to do when fully geared up in masks and flippers)
into the waters below AND followed said husband and
daughter using my combo freestyle/side style/dog paddle
(luckily I float) swimming toward the most likely spot the
sharks would be. And when said husband and daughter pick
their heads up from the water and calmly say they see sharks
I don't head back to our craft grabbing at them both. Because
a shark is a shark is a shark. BECAUSE I didn't question
or get reassured or wasn't explained to about this breed of
sharks (that were huge mind you) and their tendencies and
the ACTUAL knowledge of the "captain" of the boat and
"dive master"—I mean, yes, this is a business, these people are
trained, certified, whatever, backed up by insurance, etc., and
this is an actual "excursion" they do daily so that other people
must have survived. I'm just saying BEFORE you jump out
of a plane, don't you, besides having been taught over the last
few hours how to Do It read up, for your own satisfaction,
on your own? Plus these excursions, this particular company,
all of it was new, in this way, to Bimini. So what is it about
familial love? Whereby your daughter (knowledgeable about
all things snorkel and marine science and animal behavior, yes,
but still) asks you if you are going to "do it" (snorkel with her
and her dad and the sharks) and there is no time to question,
the boat idling, the other snorkel trip cancelled, other enthused
snorkelers waiting on you, and you Do, deaf in one ear, it
impossible to have a conversation on the way there above the
roar of the wind and the motor and just all of it, the combo
drug of the sea and the sky and the sun, too, overtaking you so
that you're dumb happy, this being what this place does to you,
but now surpassed, even, by what you think is your daughter's
joy when you said, Yes.

Flash to standing above a minnow tank as a kid spellbound, an early, early memory, as the school swam so gorgeously In Unison until one would turn, Then They All Would, the summer light flickering above them, the warmth of the day, the humming of the filter's motor. Flash to, next, standing before a bucket filled to the brim with fresh lake water, a clam placed by you, or someone you love, your mother or father, for you, in it, so you could peer at it, this seemingly nonmoving but fabulously alive thing, among those gaspingly gorgeous reflecting all myriad of oranges and greens and blues lake pebbles. Flash to a long walk you would later take through the woods on a wide path on this same stay toward some quaint clapboard shack of a store, your babysitters, really family friends, distant cousins not distant, family associated with your family, at this long-ago bought-into lake spot of deep old stocked cabins, going back many years, spun up and laughing above you, holding your and your sister's hands, to buy candy, these bark wedges or flat sticks of things you'd never seen, heard of or had before, hard, clear, bright, glassy—subdued but crystal fern green, a pale but hearkening amber, and so very sour sweet, that reflected, too, the dappling light.

And flash to, even now, the conversation you are having, mass reply all texting, with your three best friends (still, from high school) spread out across the country and one friend says she and her family are headed to "the lake," she's about to sign off to spend the afternoon on their pontoon boat and you had forgotten about pontoon boats and you are scream texting, I FORGOT ABOUT PONTOON BOATS and I DIDN'T KNOW THIS ABOUT YOU!, and OH, I'M SO JEALOUS and all these images of 70s pontoon boats soar up and Astroturf carpet and you are laughing deliriously and yelling to your family about pontoon boats and oldest daughter (who couldn't go on the Bimini trip) says I WANT TO DO THAT, I WANT TO RENT A PONTOON BOAT, HOW DO WE DO THAT? when you explain pontoon boats to her and for a brief moment you are off your preoccupation (and study of, to find out how you may have negatively impacted your family, your daughters, so you can fix it) as of late that you must be some kind of low-grade savant or in the best-case scenario some kind of changeling because you feel like a lousy mother, a lousy everything (driver, given your spatial problems, hearer, given your ear, maneuver-er with your body, given your spatial-problem-constantly-banging-into-things—hence all the bruises—listener, given your constant state of being elsewhere in your mind, the universe, whatever) but the one thing that you, during what feels like a seemingly limited amount of days or hours given how things go, but still, sometimes, can do, at least enough to keep at it, never so far give up, write, so that you get that your husband who also has his own longings including sailboats, particularly wooden Edward Hopperish style which only make you think, "crew," and, worse yet, "family crew," when your one goal upon getting on a boat is to lie down (hence the pleasure of the pontoon), seems less, well, not crazy to you, but, well, yes, you'll say it, Hard (sorry, Tom), like you (me) are hard, like your (mine) work is hard, like life, beautiful and gorgeous and the gift that it is, is, like one of my best friends texted back when I told her/them to leave me alone because I was grading (and coming down/off from our Bimini trip back into the land of S.A.D. and nonstop seven-day-a-week work to pay the bills) and she said why it's summer and I said I blippin had to, using blippin because I love my students and I'm not a grader but a responder so I hate giving grades but have to, to make money and she texted back beautifully so that I was laughing again "not blippin but fucking" and my other two best friends texted back, one after the other, "Thank you for clarifying" and "fucking Amen," after you all had reassured said friend who wrote, Thank you for clarifying, considering the at-present warning for a Tsunami to hit the Alaskan shores and she was about to impart on an Alaskan cruise in honor of her aging parents, that the cruise line would have canceled if it's really a problem, that it would all be fine, life is an adventure, yadda yadda, and, What the hell? What can it (the Articish oceans) do, throw up icebergs? Hahahahahahaha?

HEALING HOLE —*n.* 1. a. Is this it? I think.

The anxiety with its whatever pull, my hands doing their microcosm tremble. Hear me, please, some kind of warrior, I admit, I say, all along and when we reach it, swimming. I'm afraid of what I touch, can't see, can't feel, what may bite or grab my feet. It's so dark below. Not like the shallow warm ocean we just left.

b. Think, I coax, you've tried to write this before. The sheet hung up in the door. Stay with it, I encourage myself. We aren't there yet. Something cool to drink, the girl had said, a year later at her lemonade stand. Echoing her mom, I realize. Steps from where her mother kicked the ladder? Stepped off a chair (careful, listen, choose, but don't mince your words)? Now the daughter's face between the palms. Yours, you imagine, swimming, now not above the dead.

DEAR SISTER (MY CONFIDANTE) AND LIE AND LAY

Call me just tired. (I didn't sleep well last night as usual.) But all I ever want to do these days is just to lie/lay the hell down.

JUNCTURE　Today is a good day. I'm currently deluding myself into thinking late fall will not arrive. Because we will be moving. To Bimini. Where I will be writing. For a living. And my girls and husband will be doing their things. Happy as clams.

PREFACE (SEE ALSO, PREVIOUS "PREFACE")

1. The world is a serious place. Both horrible and wonderful in its seriousness. I get that. But I am just trying to have as much fun as possible. For example, for the Fourth of July in two days, I will be serving blueberries in cherry Jell-O with every kind of whipped cream variety possible: "Lite," "Regular"/ Normal, "Sugar-Free," "French Vanilla" and "Chocolate." That is, whatever I can find, have seen in the past, making it seem possible.

2. I am point blank just not going to argue with you anymore about memoir. It's needed. If it's art. I'm not saying this is but I will die if you say it's not. I'm giving it all I have. And more. My "muse" (,the word makes me cringe,) has been flying around me the whole damn time I've been writing this, on the periphery, needling, chanting, bullying, begging, coaxing. Depends on how you look at it. And I could not not listen to that woman. She's really a bitch. But the hole I'd be in in reference to the hole I was in on certain days not being able to live up to her expectations would be bigger if she did not exist. Writing can be Not Fun, but like going to the dentist, I have to do it. Some days are root canals.

3. In grad school we had to have "a language." Mine was French. I am not good at French. Everything Sedaris says is true. I am afraid of all French people, French teachers, French food, French. Add in my grad school prof for my French class was head of the "language" department. In one summer I had to learn five years of French, minus the skill of speaking it, in order to graduate. How can one do that in one class? I lived, ate, slept French. And I almost died. Eat, "do" French. Cry, "do" French. Shower, "do" French. Drive to class, "do" French. Have a nervous breakdown, "do" French. Drive home, "do" French. Stab yourself in the eye, "do" French. Lie down in the road after ordering a steamroller, "do" French. Provoke someone with a sledge hammer, "do" French. My point is. Life is serious. And my French teacher scared the shit out of me. So why do I, when I think of that class, start laughing to myself like my crazed bitch of a muse I love and abhor? Because I'm now good at French and have won awards for translating books of poetry in French? Nope. Because I did it? Yep. It also helps that I got an A.

4. This is not a preface I had the guts to put at the front of this "tome"; it is simply to say I'm glad you and I made it thus far, to here, to this book, and now, since this proem is here here, to about the middle of the book (?) (I don't know, I haven't finished writing (really, revising a million times) it yet.) Thank you. I am so proud of you for hanging in. Life is serious and horrible and wonderful and hard. And ludicrous. Thank god it's ludicrous. Tonight, on PBS, Deepak Chopra said it is the essence of paradox and contradiction, or something close. And I thank god he said that. Because, in revising this book's latest draft, I was/am feeling low. You know, root canal low. Root canal upon root canal low. Painfully low. And I needed a reminder. An essence. Break.

THE ONLY QUESTIONS I GET, AS IN ALMOST THE ONLY WORDS SPOKEN BY MY STUDENTS IN A CREATIVE WRITING CLASS I'M TEACHING TO TWELVE TO FIFTEEN YEAR OLDS, BLESS THEM:

1. How do you open this?

Me: Uhhhhh, I'm not good at opening things.

Another student: You just twist it.

2. What should I do with this?

Me: Ummm, probably keep it? I mean, do you want to?

3. Do we take these home?

Me: Yes? I mean, what? No?

4. What time is it?

Me: Not bad.

5. Where is the trashcan?

Me: Oh, yeah, I was looking for it earlier.

6. Is there a trashcan?

Me: (Truly excited and surprised): Yes! There it is! Look, there's the trashcan!

DAY 2

Student: Where do we write it?

Me: (Not sarcastically): On your paper?

Student: But we don't have any paper.

Another student, holding up paper: Yes we do, see?

Student: Shaking his head, I don't have any paper.

Me: Oh (startled), here's some paper!

Another student: You gave us paper, other students holding up paper in affirmation.

Me: Faltering, Yesterday?

Another Student: Yes.

DAY 400, I MEAN, THREE

We "do" "A&P" by John Updike.

I find myself explaining a cash register from the 70s.

Basically, I say, the "keys" were chunky,

made clunky, real sound.

The thing itself was heavy.

At this point I'm kneeling, my arm draped over the desk of a chair,

as if I'm begging it,

acting like we're already buddies,

to be my friend.

ANSWERS

I.

That I suck at teaching poetry to those who don't want to do it.

That I don't think it should even be taught when that's the case.

That I'm not going to change my mind about that.

That I think Dave Eggers wrote better describing loneliness than anyone so far I can currently remember I've ever not known.

That a man in a story picks up a locust among tens of thousands eating his crops all at once and gently tosses it back into the crowd. All I know is we were young, the teacher asked why. I'd been getting it from the first book read to me like magic. It was nothing I did. It just ran through. I said, He saw it for what it was.

2.

That I imagine in an upcoming meeting I'll have with two
other faculty, one of them being new, both of them teaching the
same classes I teach I say, Just don't hurt me.
That if I befriend you, please don't purposefully die.
That I'll spend the rest of my life having failed you. Even
though I didn't.
Fail you, that is. Yep,
I'm afraid, I'm talking to you.

DAY 8

I hand out an endearing, artful piece of fiction, the adult
author writing from the vantage point of a 12-going-on-13-
year-old boy's perspective of his grandfather telling him a story
of something traumatic that happened, to him, the grandfather,
during WWII. I pick it specifically because, not only is it art,
but I'm trying to mirror the students I teach, offer works
they'll see themselves in, be released by, inspiring them to
write. The problem is there's a part of a paragraph where the
kid describes, quite briefly, as his grandfather opens a drawer
looking for something else, that there are pornographic comic
books in that drawer, leftover from WWII. And he, the boy,
while very briefly, does describe, albeit very briefly, that there
are pictures of men in these comic books with bizarrely long
penises chasing women with their skirts ridiculously lifted
by their running, or, perhaps, the wind. And so when I get to
that passage, I panic for a second realizing it's there, that I'd
forgotten, as I tell the students we aren't going to read that
paragraph and I skip, almost without missing a beat, to the
next one and keep reading. As I said, the narrative doesn't
turn on these sentences or even refer to them. I think it's just
a way for us to learn that the boy knows what he knows,
he'll understand, on some level, a deep one, the trauma the
grandfather experiences along with others because of the war
and how this reflects our entire world. Like my teen students
know what they know. But still, having been so excited to

bring in the work that I think will move and change my students for the better, therefore even knowing it intimately, I forget these sentences are there. And not appropriate for older middle school, young high school students, whether they know it or not. So the problem is, in this particular case, I can't land on what's right to do, not given what I know, but considering protocol. I mean, I know what I want to do, even in an imperfect world. I want to respect the integrity of the story, the integrity my students have or could potentially and let it go resting with the hope I had before that this story will inform their creative lives that they are so knee-deep in trying to let escape, create and in some cases, given the demands of the world, aren't able to get out—and conceivably, this just means, aren't letting out *yet*. As a consequence the piece, all two pages of it, tumbles around in my mind. Bangs away and heats up. Like shoes in a dryer. Kicking the door open. Filling the house with silence. The job still not done.

WAXING AND WANING At 73 my

mother is unimpressed with my life. She is above and beyond
"all this busyness" which she accuses of the world behind us, an
eventual cityscape, beyond shore, that seemingly includes me.
We are at the beach and in front of us lands whom I consider
to be more than a ragged seagull. It's Jonathan. He looks back.
Watches us with a seeming knowing air.

I get my mother. But I also consider the way I help raise my
children and most of what else I do and the way I do it and
with whom (Tom) why I'm here on earth. So I comment but
then go back to my quiet book, move in, while the ocean, that
giant machine, washes every shell, piece of trash, mammal,
plant, stone and bone. And then even sometimes tosses it up.

CLUES   My husband and I leave each other clues.
There's the new t-shirt draped carefully over the washer: Wash
and let air dry once so it won't shrink. The empty box placed
prominently: We need more. The little bags of dog food: You
know I hate making decisions. The bottle of shampoo left
at an angle near the bathroom sink: This one's not working
for me, you? The burned out light bulbs not replaced: Eh.
Sometimes there're assertions, bottles in a row turned upside
down, wedged between things so they won't fall. Laundered
socks without mates, draped for months, years? (it's happened),
over the banister. My favorite is the GPS, cords organized and
wound, left near the door: I don't know where you're going
but I don't want you to get lost.

CLUES II   I swear to god what can get me to go
do laps at the gym we can't afford, once I've determined
everything else is, for the moment, at a standstill or safe, is
not that the water is Extremely warm or that the indoor pool
(it's winter, People) is under a glass roof (both godsends), that
it will calm my normally overly anxious state or make me
live longer (do any of us truly believe this? that it will trump
everything else working against us? enough at least to get us
past rationalization?), but the possibility that, near the blow
dryers and past the towels, on the counter by the overly large
and too availably positioned all-encompassing gargantuan
mirror among many the same in the women's dressing room,
there might be samples that are free.

JUPITER/MAN IN THE MOON

Recently I heard how one of the moons of Jupiter might actually be the sole place in our solar system conducive to life—or our kind of existence, I guess, not human, obviously, but you know what I mean, a cell or two, or some gases good for making them, swirling above a science-ish pool. Think of it, you, not quite a reflection of a mien, looking at something you can't howl at or blame for craziness and crime. Living way bigger, in your face, love so apparent that it is emptiness too.

TRANSITION   I haven't been home alone overnight for more than 20 years, and so it happens that tonight I will, my husband out of town, the last daughter on a whim with friends deciding to drive to the coast in a fellow parent's heavy black luxury car. I see them leave. After trying to help said daughter find a beach towel. Among other things. That she ends up finding herself.

(SUPER)MOON II   One daughter, there in
spirit, for she has done an amazing painting, seemingly out
of nowhere, of a jellyfish, this summer, before we leave for
my husband's, their dad's, their great grandmother's and
grandparent's place where one night of supermoon, up the half
block, up again trudging slowly in the dark, the wide sand
path packed down with gleaming pebbles, and lined by newly
planted tufts of grass, row upon dizzying row spanning as far
as one can see to the left and right, we crest seeing the huge
wide pregnant swath of moon on sea as if the ocean gifted itself
with a separate beam, and, then, closer, those disks, jellyfish,
awash, stilled, as glittering thick pucks, so that even the words,
"disk" and "pucks," are onomatopoetic, the fish having been
coated by sand, both sides, the daughter here, her being, all
things good/animal/marine, the other daughter's painting
circling back, as if on water, as if by hand, as we speak, the
girls' grandfather, father, and I, choosing or not, allowing the
life to do its thing, suspend, cycle down or live, scoop the jellies,
one by one or two by two or three by three as if we are waiters
or servers balancing little plates along our arms as we move
toward the I-hope-forever gently sliding back and back, as in
gold daylight on a rivulet, door upon door, then door under
door, reveal, revealed, revealing, sea.

ON BEING NAMED THE LITERARY EXEC IN A WILL OF A DEAR FRIEND FORMER PROFESSOR WHO COMMITTED SUICIDE

Of course there is no definition, handbook or encyclopedia. I know. I looked.

HOPE   The ubiquitous plastic bag. Once named
beautiful in <u>American Beauty</u>. Hung on a line of breeze. Our
last daughter's middle name.

Like I bet some of you have a kid named "Joy," or "Faith"
or something you never whispered,
until she was born.

FRIENDS   I take a picture of our takeout in the car.
Here is our dinner, I text. I take a picture of my husband
driving. Here is my husband driving, I say. I take a picture of
an intersection. Here is the intersection in our town, I write.
(By now they know I've nailed it, from far away, I've found my
tone, calmed down.) I take a picture of the car in front of us.
Here is the car in front of us, I say. I take a picture of my arm
with bracelets. Here is my "Arm," I name, "With Bracelets . . .

GIRL   Sometimes I listen to my sister like she's a god. It's been like this since I appeared ten and a half months after she was born. My post-birth self, unlike hers, being scrawny and blotched, a true newbie mess. The epitome of a tiny squall. Sure, I got cuter later, but my cuteness was deceiving. I was full-on difficult, a real pill. There is this photo of me on a couch when I'm a few days old, my body a blur, in that I'm fitfully squawking, fists and legs spun up like wheels. Sure we're in a developing country on a continent where countries are known to repeatedly topple, be violently overthrown, my dad in the CIA, but my sister, blazing a true-to-the-gut-smile could care less. And by care less, I mean it doesn't faze her because she knows she'll deal. And despite having had our parents for ten months to herself, she seems absolutely undisturbed by my presence. And since I've not known the world without her and given my temperament, I don't even go near that sturdy role, with relief. Let's shudder to think how long it took me to adjust. Hell, I'm still adjusting. In fact, I'll always have to remind myself, Girl, Look at your hands. See where you are. For example, I look down and am startled to see them gripping the wheel. I've stopped by to give her a fountain Diet Coke from Sonic (two shots of diet cherry). It's our drill. I've ordered myself the same but with one shot, and a lime. She's in her backyard. Blooming flowers doing their sway behind her. And when I say blooming, I mean gargantuan, heads. Her laptop open, she's on the phone, her oldest child's newly-rescued dog doing happy tumbles near her feet. We are both slammed. It's almost, goddamnit, fall. I fall down on the ground and do my best slapstick. Her hair, like mine, is pulled back. I scratch my foot, then roll in the grass by the dog. Pretend I'm stabbing myself. Get on all fours. I do my Frankenstein walk toward the gate. The kids next door watch suspicious. Then I act like the world is spinning. Thank you and STOP! she mouths, doubling over, pantomiming back a pretend gun to her head, as I turn the corner toward my car.

NEWS FLASH   Mom tells me that while we had
our stays in Florida between Dad's missions as CIA overseas,
once, she was freaked. Apparently Dad was doing night
training, which meant she was home alone with my sister
and me. Add in that in Nepal or Africa (I have yet to nail this
down) our house having been ransacked and my dad's tidy
alcoholism (he still managed despite his drinking to somewhat
maintain family and well maintain his job) is messing with our
mother's nerves. It's the mid 60s, Patricia's, Mom, in her early
20s, she has been to or will, as a CIA wife, several developing
countries, to birth us and have a nervous breakdown. Quite
a lot for a sheltered Catholic girl. Maybe it's just me but I feel
a storm a-brewin'. So she tips the scale and drops this little
bomb that, back then, she slept with a loaded gun. Placed
neatly under a bed in the room where we slept while Dad was
MIA (gone). Mom! I say. Then, I bet Dad loved that, trying
to make her laugh. Silence. Next, Was it cocked? She's not
sure. All she clearly offers and remembers is this: I was scared
out of my mind. And that it was so, so hot. To this day she
avoids Florida like the plague. And about it has nothing good
to say. Did David show you how to use this particular piece?
I prod. A training session? Two? She doesn't remember. Goes
on to tell me about the odd couple upstairs, how they were
"no fun," the husband also CIA, the wife came to the door
one day naked, but here's the real kicker: with an apron on.
Okay, I say, knowingly (I mean, let's be clear, we've got crazy
down on both sides), moving from the bracing image of a 60s

pinafore like apron over a naked woman's flesh all framed by the apartment building's hall to envisioning a wood floored room, two beds, dressed in cotton eyelet, up on metal frames, our toddler cheeks beet red from the heat, the pistol where she can quickly reach it, loaded, cocked. Because that's where I'd put it. Clicked in place. Neat, like a drink, or a small puzzle piece. After all, I've been trained. The apple not too far from the tree. As a kid I shot all kinds of guns. And while never toward an animal. Or a man. At cans, apples, skeet and the torso of a tree. Not that I couldn't. Because if I had to, I would, my father's goal achieved, I learned to keep my peace though it has everything to do with when, why, where, whom. And how you aim.

SIGN A MILLION, RICK MOODY'S THE BLACK VEIL   a last-minute raggedy one.

A-thrown-up-late-or-around-ten-this-morning: "Yard Sale," a small piece of scrap paper slapped over something else, understated, cryptic, "Sunday, 10-1." Like the 12 steps' fourth and fifth. It's intimidating, you just do the best you can. Or allow it to be zen-ly imperfect. Then pray. Even if it's not the way you would do it, anymore, one fell swoop to Goodwill, the stuff in big black plastic bags. Even if you are just not that up to it or in. Even if, like release, you won't truly "let go." Those secrets you harbor or have been over ad nauseam or didn't get past, the abstractly explained, tragedies "brought on" because of who I am/you are, if doing it, a fake, re-creating trauma, pass it on, then release it, take it back, be crazy, love, be loved, try not to/be ashamed.

"ACCIDENT" I describe my sister in class as bossy, because she is, In a good way, I say. She was good at running the show when we were kids and doesn't even try to boss me around or know she does it anymore. And she's saved my ass because of it. The direct and mostly indirect bulldozing. Although when referring to large equipment as a source for all things relief, we prefer the steamroller. Drive over here with it, we say, I'll be lying down in the middle of the street. The deal is my sister and I teach on the same campus, although she's a prof in the dept. of ed. So many of my students know her. In that I have a lot of education majors. And for some reason, nurses too. I think of these students when I read this amazing piece by Dave Eggers called "Accident." I'm teaching it this semester among others. Let's just say it's a little riff about loneliness and that's an understatement. My sister's presence on earth helps me fight it. But sometimes I hold it, because I'm better at loneliness than being smashed with too many people. That's the way it feels. Crashed. For example, I'm texting back and forth a little with my sister right now. Even though I'll need to stop in order to keep truly writing. Sure, I keep my door slightly ajar. My girls come and go, the dogs weave in and out, my husband potentially home, climbing the stairs. And, no, I don't savor loneliness. It's not like that. Sometimes I'm so desperate for true-blue human contact outside my family, I can weep. I mean, my mentor whom I rarely talk to and who doesn't even know she's my mentor says once unknowingly rendering a rescuer, I mean, savior, "The same for me."

HELLO, IT'S ME   You know the lyrics. It's
Rundgren. Todd. Whose stuff, to me, is mostly about his
being a commitment phobe. So why do I love, especially, those
tunes? Because I'm a glutton for punishment? Look, sure I was
attracted to the guy who in no way, shape or form was ready
to commit. And commitment's how I roll. When it comes to
men. Back then, if I was totally into you, I wanted you as all
mine. Not ironic, then, that my husband was one of Those
Guys. Even though he didn't know it. See, I was bowling with
friends. The guy who picked him up at the airport decided
to drop by. I was in this lane, as a non-bowler, at "Rock and
Bowl" (where they blast music and you go at it for a cheap
poor-college-student fee), kind of just along for the ride, in
my small university town. I turned around and he was there.
Like, one moment he wasn't and then one he was. I remember
his shirt. A rugby. Stripes of cerulean blue. Either I saw stars
or there were stars orbiting his head. My heart shot up and
wedged in my throat. And, yep, I could barely breathe. That
we're happily married now is not all you need to know. He
was Todd Rundgren and Tom Petty ("Free Falling") rolled
into one. I was up for the chase and the not acting totally like
I was. I think back to how I unknowingly coaxed him along,
how he left once for six months, how he came back, leaving a
note in poem form and a rose and my knees still buckle. That
right before I'd been driving down a dirt road. It was a full-
on Tennessee winter, as in muddled skies, torn up landscapes,
caves of snow. But when I looked up that particular night,

the sky was speckled, light. Longing, an inhabitant that had taken out a long-term lease in my throat. An ache so true and profound and dulled into submission it became clear, it was just who I was, who I'd always been, would be, in essence, who I am, that I'd come home. Let him go, I said to myself, Let him go. But I couldn't. Beauty not in contrast to what we would have but a mirror to such pain. And that's what I remember about that winter. Along with his coming back.

DEPRESSION IN GERMAN   I text my

sister, Why do I keep requesting (from the library) books in German, I say, to pick up? What am I doing wrong? I don't know, she texts. I'm at the doctor at the wrong time. And I had a conference call scheduled while I was out for a run. My phone was blowing up when I got home. Okay, I say, starting to feel better. Why does everyone drive so slow? she adds, having just ditched texting to call me since she's now in her car. Because you are a lead foot, I say. I swear to god, I'm just sitting here now listening to birds chirp. My windows down. Seriously, I say. I can't move. I'm so ding dong dang done. We try to laugh, hang up. And then I sink further into despair. Despair in German. Despair in French. Despair in every language you could ever think of. Despair in Spanish, Icelandic, Czech. Persian. Despair in Arabic. And then despair of an animal, unwritten, unsaid, unveiled, undone. Until I go inside to try and hold it enough to let it go. This grain, that. Just one.

THE JINX FACTOR (SEE ALSO, "HELLO IT'S ME") I read the entry about my husband to my husband. I never do that. Read before it, in essence, is done. Because I don't want it ruined. But I want to share it while we're driving toward a salvage place. Looking for maybe a dresser left out in the sun. Not flowers in drawers or anything. Just old or discarded. But something maybe has designs on our plans. After we leave, we get lost. The sun so eternal, open, remembering, present, not, static, forgivable, trying, imperfect, always, thank you, forget, forget, remember, gracias, anguish, I love you, there.

"OH DEAR YES OKAY" (FOR TILLIE OLSEN)   I text this back to my sister, but lower case. Then I call my mother. Mom says she and my youngest brother are headed back from Chipoltay's (her pronunciation). I'm doing my best to spell it. We share this jumbling of words. (Too many (thought?) balls in the air.) But not the sometimes shaky hands. That's mine. Actually, trembling is a better word. Even my laptop sometimes jiggles. Under my work. Like it's my first car. Fast, away. A hundred years ago. In fourth gear, fifth.   Or idle. Waiting for me to do something.

(PERFORMANCE) ART I steal a magnet off my sister's car. It says, Steve, for where we teach (Stevenson). I put it on my bumper because it's rare. I do this as a secret joke. Beth has yet to notice or punk me back. Or that's the punk. A lack of punking, her pretending she doesn't know. What I've got on the down-low. A simple test. Like with <u>Fight Club</u>: The first rule of fight club is don't talk about fight club. The second rule of fight club is don't talk about fight club. In other words, I put it back. The secret I've been leaving. Saving, as I go.

MIDDLEMARCH, AGAIN

On the news the commentator refers to the Ebola epidemic in Africa (on the Western Bulge in Liberia where I was born) as Ground Zero and I note the coined term is just almost 13 years old. Since it's September 2nd. And 11 days before our daughter was born. As proof she beautifully, at my request, emails me a birthday list, complete with links. The night before while looking for something innocuous to keep on low, I land on MTV's VMAs, and hang out there having spotted one of said daughter's favorites, Lourde. But soon it's Beyoncé gyrating among a plethora of movers and shakers. And I'm trying to understand what I'm seeing, hear the what for me is a broadside of words, Middlemarch in my lap, face down. And soon I'm Googling Beyoncé in that this is a taped performance and I'm curious as to why they are calling it the highlight of the VMAs. Is it because her significant other, Jay Z, brings their child, Blue Ivy, to the stage? The controversy over Blue Ivy's hair? Or is it because of the bootlegged leaked recorded digitized scene of Beyoncé's sister, Solange, a, perhaps, more eclectic singer, I'm told, beating on Beyoncé's beau, behind the closed doors of an elevator while Beyoncé, curiously, remains hands off, as in she doesn't intervene. Or is it because the word, "Feminist," is flashed at one point above the wealth of dancers Beyoncé has employed? In the audience, still, her daughter, and her man.

KING KONG IN LOVE

Basically, I just want you to love me. And it has to be huge. Your love. Picture this giant sculpture I saw on an institution's vast lawn. A gargantuan cherry on a spoon. You know what I mean. I'm tired of rock starry guy writers or slick chick girl writers beating me out. Ones that have way more self-esteem than I do. Or if they don't, they never silently but publically imploded in a room while the onslaught, sheer number of the gifted famous and loved students, stepped around, flat *over* them, because even if said popular writers lacked self-esteem it was cool-ish. Not needy. Not like me. Us. Look, if I'm famous, you're more famous. There's no other way about it. Because we get each other. You hearing me. Me hearing you. We work hard. We're way adults but we feel like 12. We do. Don't kid yourself. Go see that berry on that shovel. Tilted up. Toward the sky. You are that mega. You are soooooo hungry too. Like King Kong in love. You know what I mean. So vast it turns into a kind of softness whereby you can forgive everybody. Yes, even those that hurt you. Most were probably just doing the best they could. Like you. Snap a photo, you famous crying person. A colossal spoon with a whopping red cherry on it as if being lifted toward the heavens. Oh, yeah, and that yonder is freakin blue. Rock star blue. Like you. Keep that shot forever. In your mind. You giant famous person I love and adore and worship the ground you walk on. I know you.

MYSTIC(S)

Currently my mother thinks I'm a mystic. And my husband. That is, she says my husband is one too. I find this out because she emailed me to ask if my husband is a quantum physicist. I say, well, I don't think there is such a thing. I tell her he got his doctorate as an experimental physicist but beyond this and knowing he studied light, I don't have a clue. I throw in I think quantum physics is a branch. I give her his email. She says she's writing a paper for one of her classes toward earning her certificate in becoming a spiritual guide and at her last retreat she sat at a table with two people who said they were mystics. In the meantime she's been studying something to do with quantum mechanics. I warn my husband about the potential email and inform him he's a mystic. He likes the title way better than Engineer. I picture my husband in purple robes like a wizard's. A pointed hat. With gold stars. His hands on a perfect crystal ball. That is, no cracks and truly magical, like the ones I was reading about when researching thought balls while the term came to me as I was writing "balls in the air." As in too many. Or maybe it didn't come to me but when I googled "too many balls in the air" because I wanted to find the origin of the meaning it popped up. Apparently you create them by playing with the energy between your hands and when you're ready you'll have created an invisible sphere into which you can insert a thought to send to someone across space and time. But you have to be careful because you may end up messing with Karma, as in the recipient of your thought ball gets screwed up because the contract she or he signed before showing up on earth entailed things of which were going to have to get worked out. You know, payback. And they were like, "Okaaaaay, I'll do it," and signed on the dotted line knowing it'd be good for them and all of us. No matter how yuck. Or a pain in the ass. Like a step up from root canal. Like just thoroughly brushing your teeth 65,700 times. Give or take. Depending on how long you live. So you don't want to get in the way. Because that is not good. For our evolution. So I get a headache because I want to try this whole thing out—send love and healing to a dear friend who needs it in the form of a thought ball but then I get all scared I could be messing with her destiny which, ultimately, isn't her destiny but guided by my pal's free will, as in, she's here to try and "co-create," a term taught to me by my emotional energy worker. Namely, she's both here to face her Karma but also should be available to contribute to, change, uphold in a better way said Karma, being a recipient of Karma, perhaps from a past life. You know, payback. At this point, I start doing deep breathing and try out dialectical behavior therapy based on Zen Buddhism or just Buddhism (I always get them mixed up) and let the anxiety producing notions gently float by in a stream while I consider two opposites can be true at the same time in the manner of it's good to send her a thought ball and it's not good to send her a thought ball so what's the difference. I should just choose one enough already and do it. But here's the thing: So not only is "co-create" no more just a term and totally really she changed my life and helped me do it, alter the lives of others for the better, by getting me to truly be me, as in not someone based in fear but love, only so must be thought bubbles, I mean balls. Here I go with mixing up jargon. If I'm just willing to give them a try. But I'm not. Nay. Until I can

figure out what it'd mean if I sent one because I don't want
the responsibility of screwing up someone's contract, although
my eew (emotional energy worker) says contracts are broken
all the time. Maybe I just need to let go and let god. And
besides, perhaps this is where "I'll keep you in my thoughts,"
and "Sending good wishes," and the rest come from anyway.
Conceivably we know all along how to do all this stuff and/or
like my Aunt Margot says, we're born knowing but growing
makes us forget. Or same as I say to my students, you already
know what a poem is you just have to listen. Or else the whole
damn thing is about my just having too many balls in the air.
Since I have to. Because people are counting on me. To feed
them and pay for their college and teach them about poetry.
Not only people but animals. Don't get me started on our
crazy mutt rescue beautiful dogs. Who seem to see things that
aren't here. Like orbs. Akin to little light balls. Showing up on
"film." When you "record." Leave it to the digital age to help
us see our own souls. P.S. Maybe that's what Hardy was crying
out all along. We're stuck. Until we forget our destinies. And
move on.

GUN, LOADED   Yeah, we're back to the loaded
gun. Probably because I referenced one in class today. Look,
this is poetry, People. We take up dicey things. Our defense
being art. So flash on our lit weapon. The one you and I now
share. Placed, just so, for protection. Even if it's seeming. I'm
scanning the immaculately laundered white eyelet sheets, the
crafted wood floor beneath, the windows, lifted, a ways. To
let in breeze. Because of the heat. The fan, oscillating, then
pointed at us. Its gentle hum or tick, between whirrs. What
held us. All along. Air. Oh, and breathing.

REHAB   Previously a fleeting thought I'd soon forget,
this time wedged in my brain: I'm requesting my file from the
CIA. Assuming there's a file. I'll have to get back to you on
that. Maybe in my next book. Because as we know from my
last, this kind of thing takes time. Is a process. Like rehab. Like
if someone calls for you, they have to deny you're there. Once
requested, it might be a year just to get this response: there's
no one here by that name. Or, here you go, sucker, complete
with the blacked out things. But then I wonder, If you request
a file and there is no file is one automatically, after, made?
Cuz now you're a troublemaker? If you are the daughter of
someone who was in the CIA, no matter how brief, no matter
how low level, are you automatically a name on a tab of a
file on a shelf, things inside eventually photographed, made
into microfiche, scanned digital, eventually thrown in the
trash as shreds? Because, while far left, you don't amount to
anything. Noteworthy. You've never been thrown in jail. Just
suffered in silence. Empathized. Commiserated. Rescued a
few dogs. Written how you felt. Like if someone were to visit
a millennium away, earthlings having absconded, what's left
heaped, vines growing through, your progeny having ditched
for the nearest colony, spaceship or star?

SELF PORTRAIT AND CLICHÉ (SEE ALSO, DIPLOMACY AND CLICHÉ)

Dear Faculty:

I received this request today, from the administration; they want the information by Friday.

We are being asked to provide a list of all faculty, adjunct and collegiate, serving on university committees.

Sincerely,

English Department Head
University

Dear University English Department Head:

I'm on the

Avoid-the-24-hour-rule-before-sending-out-pissed-off-emails committee

and the

Despite-everything-that-kept-me-from-writing-like-thinking-
I-had-nothing-to-say-no-not-that-cuz-I-had-everything-to-
say-but-so-afraid-it-was-worth-nothing-despite-everything-
all-the-work-training-unveiling-throwing-it-away-to-get-
at-the-truth-as-in-art-not-secrets-that-are-titillating-truth-
but-truths-avoiding-cliché-as-in-an-astute-reader-asking-
who-cares?-so-making-sure-to-make-it-careable-but-that's-
of-course-way-easier-than-it-sounds-and-having-having-
having-to-do-this-relating-so-to-my-fellow-"man"woman-
and-desperately-moving-through-stupid-clinical-which-came-
first-the-chicken-or-the-egg-depression-trying-everything-
drugs-meditation-exercise-and-on-bad-reviews-or-fear-of-
potential-ones-because-anyone-can-spout-off-stupidly-and-
call-it-a-review-but-also-bad-reviews-from-those-who-know-
as-in-know-seeking-out-time-moments-even-at-Sonic-to-
write-while-hearing-out-my-students-needing-to-write-to-
live-truly-live-well-so-I-can-be-the-best-person-parent-I-can-
be-this-is-the-message-like-one-student-said-at-a-sit-in-at-a-
university-that-offered-free-tuition-for-all-but-you-had-to-
get-in-the-student-said-to-the-board-president-that-showed-
up-already-knowing-their-disbelief-that-after-spending-too-
much-on-a-building-they-had-decided-they'd-have-to-charge-
tuition-the-student-said-on-camera-this-is-your-chance-in-
front-of-the-whole-world-to-take-a-stand-and-not-only-
impact-us-but-show-the-world-it-can-be-done-like-maybe-
just-rent-out-the-building-or-something-just-take-a-leap-of-
faith-I-do-it-all-the-time-when-I-argue-and-say-no-I-have-
to-write-instead-of-being-on-university-committees-I'm-not-
getting-paid-to-be-on-nor-do-they-help-me-professionally-
nor-do-they-help-anyone-really-as-in-the-university-setting-
is-so-dysfunctional-and-I'm-an-adjunct-so-I'm-not-going-for-
tenure-and-couldn't-if-I-wanted-to-so-it-will-kill-my-spirit-

and-I-know-I-should-be-lucky-people-are-starving-but-this-is-what-I-have-to-do-to-help-us-for-now-move-forward-as-people-into-the-time-when-people-won't-starve-so-you-better-not-fire-me-but-by-god-promote-me-for-that-three-cents-more-an-hour-or-whatever-I-know-that's-why-you-asked-passively-aggressively-anyway-and-with-a-shaming-tone-for-what-"committees"-we-are-on committee

and then I'm on the

Fuck-you-if-you-think-there-are-too-many-of-us-we-need-more-artists-as-many-as-we-can-get-as-long-as-they-have-to-do-it-and-apparently-some-of-them-are-finding-that-out-right-now-given-the-economy-and-let's-be-honest-it's-not-for-the-faint-of-heart-anyway-you-try-it-do-you-see-why-I-can't-do-committees-for-now-I-would-if-I-could-and-maybe-in-the-future-if-the-world-changes committee

And, finally, the

Because-of-all-this-and-maybe-more-I-don't-get-I-always-feel-like-I'm-in-a-race-against-time-a-gun-to-my-head-writing-a-book-I'd-want-to-read-as-a-with-it-knowing-human-that-addresses-writing-sometimes-because-even-that-is-a-metaphor-like-everything-is-a-metaphor-for-everything-else-you-have-to-do-like-paint-or-play-football-or-do-physics-or-try-to-find-that-thing-you-have-to-do-as-in-part-of-your-life-purpose-it's-all-relative-it's-all-about-love-or-getting-there-I-swear-I-love-it-but-I-wish-this-were-over-too-desperately-

sometimes-just-for-a-minute-so-I-could-relish-it-just-for-a-
second-and-be-proud-before-I-start-writing-again-maybe-if-
the-muses/stars-align-once-more-and-I-have-the-wherewithal-
to-know-as-in-*know*-again-while-working-so-hard committee

DIPLOMACY AND CLICHÉ

If you just start writing and stop thinking about it, I tell my students, it will work itself out. So I try this with Mr. Chen. Ask a question like, How are you? and he would ask another and spell the answer out. Hose, he'd say, cheerfully, H, o, s, e, hose, poking at invisible letters in the air. I'd be standing outside our family housing house, my husband already in class. Former barracks, we were told, these tiny rectangular buildings, now houses, were. Lining streets that bloomed to neighborhoods despite no real encouragement, know how, trust. Where, here and there, among students, someone grew a garden, parked a stroller in the dust. So that once, probably while I watered, I saw Mr. Chen's laces somehow get caught in the mechanism of his bike that toppled, mid intersection, seemingly, the day all sky and heat, midair. Watched him get up and, I swear to god, cheerfully and quickly, as if to not be in the way, brush himself off. My heart shooting up into my throat. Mr. Chen, I couldn't help but think, was too old for this. He both looked and didn't look the part. Way older than young us. Wearing his communist clothes.

SOS/S.O.S./SIS/S.I.S.   Our joint students tell my
sister I swear a lot. Oh great, I say, Now *I'm* in trouble. With
you. A Housewife from New Jersey touting her cookbook
and paparazzi reads to the tune of hundreds, into her state-
of-the-art mic in the next-over tent. I'd warned another
reader before we showed. And that at our reading there were
liable to be only a handful, our audience, one of them drunk,
one of them belligerent, one of them desperate like us, as
in potentially crazy. I told her, you can either shout and act
your work out like some do or just get through, meaning,
give up. I tell her, that's my camp. Bail fast. Like it's raining.
Don't commune with nature. Your mind's a hotel. You are
kicking back. Because I don't know about you but the last time
someone shouted poetry at me I left feeling unwell. Look at it
this way, I offer, there'll be less chance for feedback. If we're
lucky we'll get a podium someone dragged from the street. If
we're lucky, we can rationalize it's quaint. We're *real* artists.
Last time I did this, I add, I couldn't even hear myself think.
I saw my husband in the audience with a look on his face my
sister has deemed, Stepped in Shit. His head in his hands.
Mad for me, he was gritting his teeth. I don't get it, I had said
to bait him, share the misery, one more time, a final plea for
someone to save me before I went up. I'm so confused. Sooooo
confused, I'd whispered, purred, into his ear, watching a few
possible last-minutes drag a row of our sorrowful, empty, beat
up folding aluminum chairs toward concessions so they can
sit somewhere else while consuming their organic sausages

(Organic? Why bother?), downing their locally handcrafted beers with names like Smoked Sapling (Give me a break). Then I *really* focus, salvage what's left of the day by organizing something, culling two stray socks, put them on, when we get home, letting it all in at last. Set back on the periphery despair. What's more I do what saves me. I love it. Try to let it love me. And I laugh and laugh and laugh.

HUNTERS AND GATHERERS   Look,

they'll have already started folding into themselves before they enter the house. Upon their different arrivals, I want them to see the kitchen counter as a complete display. The packaged sandwiches, options, labeled who's for what, according to their needs and likes. Bakery cookies. Chipotle flavored chips. Freshly ladled into containers soup. So they can pick. Because this is what I'm good at. I mean, what if everything you do and believe when you work so hard and reach some sort of state is art because you don't know it is but you are trying to go for that state because you know that it's real, a state of right and good, no, not right, beyond right, just good? So, like with food, most nights you (and your husband or wife or partner if this applies) can't cook, so for your family to eat because you're lousy at killing it at anything, anymore, or at least you now know, and don't want to identify, you never were?

SNOW EVENT   They make it funny, my students,
the frenzy, replacing "storm" with "event." Like it'll entail
tickets and popcorn as we slide home in our cars. Or towards
grocery stores where the shelves will be depleted, stripped
bare, as if this is it, the second coming, or the end of the world,
either way, many fearful they're screwed. And the way, in
turn, a cartoon replaces pain with stars, or like the swirling, I
swear to god, the first time I saw my husband, around his head,
the bowling alley and all its song and news receding, like the
snow's whiteout and shutdown otherworldly, we say, at the
apex in the night of the storm, under streetlights, minus stars.
Super slow mo we used to call it, when watching football, and
they'd spin the guy back and start over so we could see him
carefully in his mistake or winning catch or pass. It was either
that—football for those of us not interested, or, on the other
channels, watching snow. So study we did how they did it, how
it was, for them, to be alive. Be *grounded,* I'd admonished, to
myself, turning back from my future husband that first time I
saw him, stunned, so bright were the stars, grounded the word
my mother used to get control, say for now you're not going
anywhere, when we knew it was only a matter of time, being
that we were, like my father who'd left, in love with the whole
wide world.

SILENCES, EXTREME COUPONING, POETRY (SEE ALSO, GROUNDLINGS/ONE ART/NO ART)   Like my niece says to me, I can't think in appropriate words. I hate poetry and poems and poets. And let's throw in elite schools. I'd be better as an extreme couponer. Or, right now, on my own reality show. The Housewives of Poetry. I can picture myself barely avoiding a brawl. I don't want to argue anymore about who is more self-absorbed than whom. Conveyed by who writes what and how. That it takes all kinds. Yeah, it does. So some of us can be groundlings for those whisked right onto the stage. Streamlined right into not affordable (for us) elite schools, except the three in history who had their acts together, young enough, as if somehow more than human, overcoming terribly debilitating factors like illness and poverty and class and bigotry and low self-esteem and self-fulfilling prophecies, for once and for all, or long enough, to know what it would mean to get into a really good school. So they do. And these guys deserve it. They do. Ah, for the next life, I tell myself. (Except for my girls. For whom I'm hell bent.) Or maybe it's all about just a certain tude (my sister's perfect word) that I don't and never will have given that I'm the notorious poster child for low self-esteem, that is, incapable of rock-star smooth, or one loved, in general, by rock-star smooths. People, at 50, I'll still wear my heart on my sleeve. Furthermore, I don't know if I'm into the climb and the lessons anymore. Because I can't shut up. I've spent almost the whole time afraid and/or just wanting to be loved minus a hiatus or two. So fuck everything in my world but whom I love or could potentially love once I/if I were to/if I could meet them, that is, you, yes, I'll say it, if you *get* this, *really get this*, except, as I said, and, okay, those of you who don't, I'll try, I'll try, bless you, thank you, even though I don't know you, Love, I love you, too (unless you don't want me to). P.S. Lighten up, I need to let off this steam so if you are mad at me right now I'm fucking sorry for being a simpleton and thinking there's this easy category of people/poets I can throw under one bus. I'm low, people, low. Okay, so I retract what I said, I'm sorry, I get it, it's me, I'm lame, my bad, I'm sorry (but I'm still a little pissed), I love poetry and poets and poems. I love all of you, everything, again, but maybe evil/people, if there is such a thing, as in evil hasn't just taken up residence in them, whatever evil is (or not . . .

MAUS

Until my friend Jenny said to me, Well, have you read <u>Maus</u>? Then, it's about the holocaust, I didn't know. I mean, I don't read comic books, except for a brief period when I consumed Archie's around fourth grade. Now *there's* an agenda. But anyway, these, <u>Maus</u> <u>I</u> and <u>II</u>, are technically graphic novels, this genre courageously rising up in recent decades but still somewhat news to me. I mean, I never kept at it, the art, likewise I never knew to make the leap. So I'm up all night reading books <u>I</u> and <u>II</u>, stumbling the next day into class. I tell my students about it, assuming they'll already know, being mostly young and hip, in tune with all things, well, new. They blink blankly at me. Only one slowly raises her hand: I think I've heard of it. So I guess it's not just me. I decide, There's just so much out there that's good. In that, I'm afraid I'll never get to it all. Of course I won't get to it all.

But maybe that's the point.

I'm sorry, world, I say, I've been such a bitch. For days.

Until last thoughts before I sleep, I wish I could fucking draw. . .

GROUNDLINGS/"ONE ART"/NO ART (SEE ALSO, <u>SILENCES</u>, EXTREME COUPONING, POETRY)

I'm anticipating the end. The end being this book you are reading. Way huge, in that here come the *celebrated* critics. As in, These People Have Names.

I've cleaned the house (something I'm extremely good at) in preparation. Because this may send me, we say in my family, Off the Deep End (to bed for days). And I like a clean house when I'm (immobile) "re-grouping" (something else we also say). People, I prepare. Here are the transcripts from the meeting I'll run like a song. Set on auto. Replay. After all, you are entering my brain: Where's Elizabeth? I ask. She couldn't make it, they say, snickering (You think you are worthy of her? No way). Besides, we got it covered. What about Francine? I'll push. She's busy, they report after a pre-game huddle (literally shoving down their guffaws so that they almost choke). Okay, I sigh, like I have a right, booting up the slide show: Every Stupid and Humiliating Thing I've Ever Done, in lieu of but in association with, my actual work. Then we sit back. And get no further. They leave, I crawl into bed for said days. Except for to teach, "make" dinner, sometimes get the mail.

Until I get up, come here anyway.

Because I have to.

Welcome to our world, part deux.

CONTEMPLATIVE SPICE   I lose another award and the grant manager tells me the jurors gave my work highest marks but my narrative of a budget was too vague. She says, kindly, You just need a spreadsheet. Because I'd simply put, in so many words, I'd take the money, get the hell out of here and head south. To finish my book, I'd added, weakly, in the addendum. Sure, I admit, nowwww, I sound like a desperate unarmed freak of a bank robber asking for permission. But I didn't know what else to posit and thought more would be insulting. I mean, when I do these apps, sometimes I'm cold and sometimes hot. So I didn't do it, what I thought they didn't ask: A plane ticket equals this. A hotel stay this. I guess I could have thrown in a letter from my doc: Yeah, the girl has S.A.D. Bad. One of the worst cases, if not The Worst, I've ever seen. She can go down the tubes like the itsy bitsy spider in a flash, even one of those dark wet days in full summer. And it gets worse every year. Because she's used up her reserve. Even to the point of not being able to feel her body parts. Shit, going back over all this and the prospect of the next 7 months makes one have to lie down. But didn't somebody recently talk about being bedridden and managing only a sentence a day of her now world-renowned book? But I have a family to love and money I gotta make, I counter to that thought. And love requires movement around here. Go figure, money's the same. So since it's fall I contemplate spice. If I were a Spice Girl, I'd name myself, Way Downer Spice. Wear black. Stick with ballads. I mean, as we speak, pumpkins are being plunked on porches, people are slapping cornstalks on anything vertical. Yay Fall, I say under my breath, going for irony, as in, literary, in my best rock star cool tude voice for the pretend camera in the car, the invisible documentarian traveling with us for this book, giving me a reason other than I have to for writing on my worst days, making me accountable, while driving past, waving, thumbs up. I mean, clearly, I need you to sing.

A SURREAL SELF-PORTRAIT
SERIES   Literary memoir with eyes, literary memoir with eyes, literary memoir with eyes, literary memoir with eyes, literary memoir with eyes, literary memoir with eyes.

YOU IMAGINE THE WORST, LIKE CORMAC, THAT TURNS INTO THE BEST, LIKE CORMAC, COMMONPLACE BOOK ENTRY THAT MATTERS WHEN YOU ARE HUMAN AND ON THE LAM IN A POST-APOCALYPTIC WORLD:

"No lists of things to be done. The day providential to itself. The hour. There is no later. This is later. All things of grace and beauty such that one holds them to one's heart have a common provenance in pain. Their birth in grief and ashes. So, he whispered to the sleeping boy. I have you."

—Cormac McCarthy, <u>The Road</u>

BEING FOUND   I send my sister an email like this

and she returns an email like this

what?

and I return an email like this

nothing

and she returns an email like this

I know

WRITING. WHEN YOU CAN'T.
It rains then snows then rains on the snow that isn't beautiful.
You describe the fog that ensues as tattered. An envelope. The
beard of a gnome. Beneath it you imagine funky shrooms.
Alice. A red coat. Falling down a hole. You stick with that
image. Fall down your life. Don't weep. Go past see. Past God
and Job and geese flying south or returning, a fist. There's your
husband in winter the night you first saw him. He has a scarf.
You don't. It's not the ending and beginning. What gives. It is
more than real.

This is not why.

But it helps.

I TEACH MY STUDENTS ABOUT FOUND POETRY

Then Mom calls. Says she saw an old picture. That she'd never seen before. A friend's. Of her and Dad. He's sober. And everything comes back. What was right and new. A marriage, she offers. It was a real marriage. We had so much fun. Before. She doesn't want to leave it. Sitting there on her couch. It comes in waves. And the light and warmth too. She asks my father, seemingly of the air, Well, can you help me with this? And my father, he's grateful. Flies around, sometimes to a soar, says something, anything, everything like before there was no more.

"ROAM IF YOU WANT TO, ROAM AROUND THE WORLD" Sweet sister

luck, last night our youngest daughter saw a fox, far out, in tall grass, when we went looking for our dog, all four of us, separate, in our cars. It turns out he (our lost guy) was close to home, two houses up, enjoying a steak dinner. And I know he wasn't afraid. As long as he's with a good human, he's fine. Our youngest either. She said she knew we'd find him, the fox a sign. So this girl, among us all, remained the most sure. When we got him home, Sandy (our now found four-legged), licked our faces clean and easily settled back in. My husband went to bed. And I picked up the remnants of the scare—leftover flyers, rolls of packing tape, pushpins, discarded printer cartridges, water bottles, empty, drained, extra collars, a leash and put blankets over our oldest, now on the couch, sunk in sleep, her face swollen from crying, mascara smeared, the universe having coughed our guy up, so what we come back to is what we know, we moved through the night deeply. And, as it happens now, we can roam, breathe.

CASPER 's not an orb. I mean, bless him, he's friendly and everything. But orbs I have seen. And Casper, he's no orb.

Just saying.

GODSPEED   As if I'm holed up doing a labyrinth or
on a retreat and way not into it but don't want to fail whatever
it is I'm supposed to "learn" in jail/doing time, god says to me
via cell (smuggled in or used on the sly) concerning the crisis I
don't want my daughters to pick up on, Let's just get through
not losing your mind.

GOING TO SKYWRITING IN MY MIND

Library books back/up

House

Yard

Longing

Store

ISH   By now you know I consider ish a word and a gift. I tell my students the more specific, the more universal. But that rules are made to be broken. Because I believe this probably more. The defeated part earned, the scrolling credits of a great film, the quiet shuffling, those who choose to stay seated rising in the dark when they are finally compelled by duty, convention, or the chain of events that lead to it, hopefully, love, or some other brilliance near.

OK   That blue light with wisps of dust cone-ing out,
Beckett being his way avant-garde self I love, the old woman
in his play, filmed, in black and white, rocks and chants
something dark. I'm thinking, Okay, I get this. Later, my
thesis advisor emerges from the projection room, on crutches
for an injured knee, laughing, says it was the perfect place to
nap. Then a plate of food, before us, each, a sheaf of my poems
to my left she's read, she says, No, don't. I'm about to start
over again, throw all I've written away. Instead I cock my ear.
Listen. Ok, I say, finally, nodding, tears, relief I'm alive to hear
this, my husband with our child not far away.
Ok, ok, ok.

HOW TO FEEL BETTER IN SO MANY WORDS

At the beach, day three, to fight
my S.A.D. and write, I see the woman my husband and I have
termed the laughing lady, two glorious soon-to-be shaking off
black dogs, a mid-size heron fill up his bill, a topless woman,
great body, who places her hands just so, wafts in smelling of
weed, and picks a spot among men, as if she doesn't know,
and a cool wooden ship, restored, three masts, that fires off a
pretend cannon scaring the bejeezus out of us on shore. We
actually fall out of our chairs. (I scream, then laugh.) I can see
the silhouettes of people on board high five each other, I swear.
Or maybe that's all in my head. Regardless, in my thinking,
I'm not alone.

ROCKET   Like David Shields says to me in an email,
it isn't the guy's book itself that is his greatest achievement,
it's his website, devoted to quoting the rejections he got.
Careful, or he will cite ya, someone must have said. Because
they *are* entertaining. Those rejections. Ongoing. There's
no end. This pissed off guy, he will just not let go. Which is
his greatest talent. And that he won't take no for an answer.
Finally published, his book, he wants made into a film. His
life *is* art, I agree. But still I'm not sure we are on the same
plane. To rocket yourself, and scream, like a magnet, toward
a steel sun. Beautiful, yes, but there's the crash. It's like he's
sacrificing himself for us. I mean, I commiserate, he's real. And
I appreciate it and everything. Even want to cheer him on. But
what is so futile about it. Going after a dream. He makes me
feel its futility. Until the end of time. And I don't need to do
that. I want to hearken to the other, maybe the essence of it,
bless him, his dream. This is when I'm, albeit fitfully, there.

POUND (EZRA) AND CRAFTS

I obviously can't quote the whole thing here but the poem I'm thinking of, Pound's, has to do with leaves, a bough which is black and wet, and upturned faces. I'm nuts about that lyric, grateful that I knew it today, and yesterday, and the day before, in the fall rain. And I mention this in my last book but I think my mom and Ezra share one major thing. They both spent time at St. Elizabeths (a federal psychiatric hospital). But Mom's hiatus was brief. She'd been whisked from overseas (Nepal) having had a "nervous breakdown" (my alcoholic dad was in the CIA, she birthed two babies ten months apart, one of them being me, in northern Africa, she was, like, 23, it being the early 60s, she was having panic attacks (go figure) . . . —Look, just see my last book, My CIA, for more info.). While Pound's stay was the result of things much dicier, relatively speaking, in that, depending on how you look at it, and if you Are the CIA you can look at it much more seriously, as in a broken spouse is a potential leak—but, anyway, Ezra said some not borderline not good things via Italy and Mussolini-ish stuff and such was attributed to him cracking up, while my poor beautiful mother basically imploded from aforementioned stress. Anyhoo, I like to think that, while not being a great thing to have shared, at least, I'm sure, from my mom's point of view, Pound and Pam (Mom's name) could have been near bunkmates. Hell, my mother's an artist too. Can you imagine the conversation? Two "crazy" artists in an exchange? Okay, not bunk mates but maybe "ward" mates. Okay, maybe not

"ward" mates but floor mates. Building mates? Lawn mates?
So perchance they only saw each other at lunch. Regardless,
soon enough my mother was hurried out and hurtled home, to
the Midwest, where she would take up her life raising me and
my sister plus eventually our two brothers while, at least at
first, Dad went off overseas. So back to Pound's leaves. I
imagine a myriad, pale greens, wet beiges to raucous orange. In
fact, I'm sitting on a train right now in my mind, looking out
the window, like Pound, upon those faces upturned. Maybe on
the ground these slick leaves he associates them with, almost
glittering like we used to make, as girl scouts or Brownies or
campers when I was a kid, gluing them to a "plaque"
furthermore slicking afore-mentioned fronds and the whole
rough, splintery board smooth with a thick coat of varnish or
shellac so they could shine to what for us was forever. Glossed.
In the realm of Martha Stewart and her spray paint. Gold on
acorns, pinecones, sticks, leaves and even nests, but better. Kind
of like I plan to do to this particular manuscript, shine it up—
one, which is, at this point, still a mess, until, that is, you see it
(hopefully). Anyway, I've decided my next move, when this
whole thing is done, pieced together, corralled, rearranged,
smudgy notes, addendums and arrows peppered throughout,
when it's still a just-before-the-final draft huge thick stack,
bound only by a giant black clip, is to drop it in the center of
our wood-floored bedroom impactfully, this part being
performance of performance art, no one around, with a thud,
and snap a photo of the disheveled manuscript to paste up on
my "website." Announce, This is it! Soon! To my zero
followers, I'll say, Drool, slobber, feast! Or just plain, Let your
eyes gaze. Kind of like post-op. An organ or two repaired,
healing still to be done—or maybe the mind with shock. Like

Pound coming to terms if he did. Like my mother, years later,
way down the track, speaking, divine, That it wasn't her fault
in the first place.

FRIENDS   At a local convenience store I have two, especially, friends. I tell my girls, to whom regional friendships are important, that, much to their dismay, in this town I'm too introverted for more, just to get a rise out of them. Ironically the one of the two clerks to which I'm closest I don't understand except when catching small phrases. She's Russian or from one of the former Russian countries and I don't mean to be insensitive but I didn't want to ask her to repeat a third time since her accent is so strong. She's stereotypically gruff. Says everyone is a crook. One time I accidentally handed her a nickel instead of a quarter and she slammed the money down on the counter calling out what I'd done as if busting me mid scam. I can't see, I said, I'm deaf in one ear. That was the first time we met. Then I laughed. And, eventually, so did she. But it looked unnatural. As though the woman had to remember how. It was probably high summer. An older Russian gal coming from the bowels of a country seemingly democratic but portrayed as majorly corrupt after years of iron rule, at least to Americans. I could see her denouncing something, fist in air. So we were friends. I had seemingly tried to put one over on her. In the form of twenty cents. I found myself doing easy little tasks to please Russian lady. Like having out ahead of time the exact right change. Ask her about Putin and she'd go off on a tirade. Shout, He is a crook! planting herself in the middle of some demonstration under a dour sky, folks wrapped around an ugly building, in line for a few grocery items, a smattering of beheaded frozen fowl, alone in a cavernous, gaping freezer, to choose from. God help ya, my sister warned, when we first moved locally, if you ask for assistance at the other place she worked. Don't get lost or you'll never get out. And that's the thing. I imagine this woman's route to now: Small municipality. Mid Atlantic East Coast. Why I feel I'm closer to her than the other guy I converse with at what my family and I have affectionately dubbed The Corner Store I don't know. The other employee is young. A boy, I consider. Fresh out of IT school and can't find the position he wants. High school to post college to here, the guy's worked this same job. But he's obsessed with and incredibly knowledgeable concerning the weather. Tracking it, knowing how, when and why whatever is bad is about to appear. I swear he looks as though he's about to lift off when a blizzard, hurricane or major thunderstorm potentially spawning tornadoes is near. Weeks before, let's call him Holden, will give me the five different possible scenarios of the coming squall and name the one most likely. And here I can also depend on the prospect of their fountain Diet Coke. To not be wonky, distasteful or out. Exceptionally low in winter, I'll hazard the energy in order to talk. Holden's nonexistent girlfriend is so not waiting in the wings, he's told me. She'll get there, I've offered, because I believe. Likewise we get through. I mean I figure it's one of the reasons I'm here. I guess life purpose kicks in. I like that he values an ear. Although when I'm especially exhausted I have to start talking myself up. Sometimes I'll get back in the car, diet caffeinated soda in hand, sucking it down, taking my medicine, reading my daily meditation for crackups post talk and feel like I've climbed a mountain to the moon, the relief so palpable.

KEY WEST   In Key West, I see two iguanas, one of which appears two days. I dub her Shauna the Iguana. Text pictures to our daughters. She's feisty, this one, I say. Falls from a palm tree. Unfazed, climbs back up. In a close-up, her back is all iridescence. Among flowers, she eats leaves. Rustling signals she's here. I admit I want to feel her spine. Study her iridescence. Sometimes blue. Sometimes green. When she moves in the sunlight there's change.

<u>MY CIA</u> So recently I was invited to read from my last book, a memoir as you know, <u>My CIA</u>, and when I'm done this guy asks, What happens at the end? In front of everybody. All three people in the audience. I balk. I feel dizzy. There is nothing, I say, with a shrug, a wave of the hand, as though I'm dismissing everything. But not including him.

BAT OUT OF HELL   My sister passes me like a bat out of hell. She doesn't know it's me. I call her. I am laughing. You just passed me like a bat out of hell, I say. I thought you were turning left! she yells, I didn't know it was you, plus You had your blinker on! Oh, I say, Whoops, I must've had it going for miles. Another car roars past and slams into the lane between her and me neatly like the sound of a turning lock. See! I shout, affirming her, It's always me that's wrong! Then because I've caught her she tells me about a dream. We were in our beds under mosquito nets (Nepal) and I was crying to get out. She undoes mine. I crawl next to her. She goes, You were like a little monkey the way you crawled. I love this image. As if an appendage, a fellow mom once said describing her daughter always hanging on. We're driving in cold and rain. Eventually she takes a left. We hang up. Three days. Three days, I give myself, before I grab my family, load the car, and scram.

DREAMING IN HORSES/FULL DISCLOSURE, PART I

There's something I haven't told you, haven't wanted to tell you, like it's real, like, as in the 12 Steps I'm doing the fifth—about to tell you some bad thing I did. I dream in horses. The same horses. Two definitely, maybe three. In stalls in a shed next to a house we used to live in. But in my dreams I forget. Startle to, remembering. They need to be let out. They need water, food, to be groomed. In the dream I tell myself this is because we inherited the horses. With the house. In the dream I watch myself terrified, at a run, find their buckets empty, and yet they still look at me as horses do, out of some vastly good emptiness we often call love, and I'm weeping, weeping, I'm so sorry, Thank you, thank you. I let them out. I fill their buckets to the brim, put down fresh hay, gently wash them down. And once awake know again nothing about horses except maybe what I saw myself just do. Then there's the story of my husband, how I dream him, and our girls, and how a friend of a friend steals from us in the shop of a hotel. How I'm left with nothing, they are gone, I'm trying to rectify, crying, Not them, I'm sorry, what did I do, forget, not know, not them. There is no end to this. This dream. It's something I live with, have come to live with, for so long. I've tried to figure it out. For so long. Why the punishing dreams. And then I think it's just that I'm alive. That being alive is not enough. Being human. There is something else, better, to be. And that I must know it. I love it. I long for it. Somewhere, there. But I know I'm supposed to, or want to, say something different. But I cannot. Because of my girls and my husband and my family, my brothers, my gone father, my mother, my nieces, my sister, my brother-in-law, my husband's parents and family (mine now), all my mentors in moments or vastly (dianne, Marianne, k, David, Karen, Mc . . .), my students, and our animals, all the animals I see.

GLOSSARY   After whatever "English book"
we were using in elementary school, my favorite was social
studies. I'd pour over that thing and embrace the ensuing
crafts. The glossaries chocolate icing, words bolded plus
defined in kid language, later would save your ass in history
when the teacher handed out a massive packet of badly copied
worksheets forcing you to belly up to the bar of boredom, an
endless blazing *cartoon* (otherwise you'd be dazed and it'd be
great) sidewalk where you were filling in cracks. If you were
lucky there was a glossary. Because maybe it was too late,
the writers of your text considering such childish, that you
should be too smart. So then you'd go to the index. Last resort
being to read what you considered boring and/or suspicious
"crap." Because even then you could smell a rat. History de-
emphasized the truth. And you were invested in other scams.
Rebel too much and you'd be Rick Moody's dead girl or Toni
Nelson's <u>Nobody's</u>. Thus you skimmed for all unless it was
underground. And concentrated on things like your hair.
Worried not about who you were in love with but who was
in love with you. Because, you felt, despite what the teacher
said, it made no more sense, when you broke it apart or down.
So much that you got the message, held to your heart the two
endings, one leading to the other, boat to light to pier to green
to boat, and passed the note, because there would be love and
beauty and truth and hope. And you still had some things to
figure out.

REAL GLOSSARY of things referred to,

alluded to or referenced in the preceding but unfortunately not further defined here. Also, this is not a complete list

The CIA

Pound's leaf poem

The Great Gatsby

Beauty

Catcher in the Rye

Love

Cat's Eye

Keats' famous urn poem

Truth as a person who changes his mind a lot, depending on her mood, but in a truthful way

Kali

Roam if you want to, roam around the world

Guns

"Feeling Fucked Up" by Etheridge Knight

Seasonal Affective Disorder

Craft(s)

Rehab

That bitch I call a/my muse. (It's okay, we have that kind of a relationship.)

D. M. Steele

And, again, *Roam if you want to, roam around the world* . . .

Katherine McCord's two books of poetry are *Island* and *Living Room* (prose poems). Her third book, *My CIA*, is a lyric essay/memoir. *My CIA* was named a top ten book of 2012 by the *Review of Arts, Literature, Philosophy and the Humanities* and added to their ongoing list of great nonfiction reads. It won a Baker Artist Award; was showcased on Maryland Public Television's *An Artworks Special*; and was featured through an art installation co-produced by Maryland Institute College of Art's MFA in Curatorial Practice in early December 2013 in Baltimore. She has published widely in literary journals and magazines such as *APR*. She has an MFA in Poetry and an MA in English/Creative Writing/Poetry. In 2011 and 2014, McCord won Maryland Individual Artist Awards (state grants in creative writing). She has been awarded finalist/semi-finalist status in the Emerging Writer Fellowship Competition, The Writer's Center, Maryland; the Joaquin Miller Cabin Reading Series, Washington, DC; the Autumn House Press Open Competition; The "Discovery"/*The Nation* Poetry Contest; the *Poet Lore* Narrative Poetry Competition; The Chester H. Jones Foundation National Poetry Competition; *The Maryland Poetry Review* Poetry Contest; and the fellowship competition, Summer Literary Seminars in Lithuania and Kenya, 2013. She teaches Creative Writing at Stevenson University and the University of Maryland University College. Finally, recently she won the Gabehart Prize in (Creative) Nonfiction for an excerpt from her manuscript, *RUN SCREAM UNBURY SAVE;* was named one of three finalists for the Tony Quagliano International Poetry Award; and was awarded a Hoffer Legacy (Creative) Nonfiction Award for *My CIA*.

previous winners of the
autumn house nonfiction prize

Love for Sale and Other Essays by Clifford Thompson, 2012, selected by Phillip Lopate

A Greater Monster by Adam Patric Miller, 2013, selected by Phillip Lopate

So Many Africas: Six Years in a Zambian Village by Jill Kandel, 2014, selected by Dinty W. Moore

Presentimiento: A Life in Dreams by Harrison Candelaria Fletcher, 2015, selected by Dinty W. Moore

RUN SCREAM UNBURY SAVE by Katherine McCord, 2016, selected by Michael Martone

design and production

Cover and text design: Chiquita Babb

Author photograph: Courtesy of GBCA

The text of this book is set in Granjon, a font designed by George William Jones (1860–1942) in 1928. The old-style serif typeface was based on the sixteenth-century typeface Texte, designed by Claude Garamond (1480–1561).
The display text is set in Fragment Core, designed in 2011 by Shuji Kikuchi

Printed by McNaughton & Gunn on 55# Glatfelter Natural